BLOGGING LIKE A NINJA

Making Money on Blogging

Starting from Scratch

-

The Definitive guide for beginners

(Best Blogging Books and Audiobooks – book1)

By Dave Connally

© **Copyright 2020 by Dave Connally**
All rights reserved.

This document is geared towards providing exact and reliable information with regards to the topic and issue covered. The publication is sold with the idea that the publisher is not required to render accounting, officially permitted, or otherwise, qualified services. If advice is necessary, legal or professional, a practiced individual in the profession should be ordered.

- From a Declaration of Principles which was accepted and approved equally by a Committee of the American Bar Association and a Committee of Publishers and Associations.

In no way is it legal to reproduce, duplicate, or transmit any part of this document in either electronic means or in printed format. Recording of this publication is strictly prohibited and any storage of this document is not allowed unless with written permission from the publisher. All rights reserved.

The information provided herein is stated to be truthful and consistent, in that any liability, in terms of inattention or otherwise, by any usage or abuse of any policies, processes, or directions contained within is the solitary and utter responsibility of the recipient reader. Under no circumstances will any legal responsibility or blame be held against the publisher for any reparation, damages, or monetary loss due to the information herein, either directly or indirectly.

Respective authors own all copyrights not held by the publisher.

The information herein is offered for informational purposes solely and is universal as so. The presentation of the information is without contract or any type of guarantee assurance.

The trademarks that are used are without any consent, and the publication of the trademark is without permission or backing by the trademark owner. All trademarks and brands within this book are for clarifying purposes only and are the owned by the owners themselves, not affiliated with this document

Table of Contents

Introduction 1

Chapter One: Can I thrive as a blogger? 7

Chapter Two: Starting a blog? 11

Importance of Blogging and 10 Ways of Increasing Targeted Traffic............................ 23

Chapter Three: Getting started 31

    First things first – choose a niche 32

    What is a niche?.. 34

    How to find a blog niche? 38

Chapter Four: which blogging platform to use? 58

    What is WordPress.. 61

    Domain name 63

Chapter Five: Getting relevant content for your blog... 74

Chapter Six: Writing an intriguing blog post? 91

Chapter Seven: what you need to know about SEO (Search Engine Optimization) 100

Chapter Eight: Monetize your blog............... 111

Chapter Nine: Means of Blog monetization – Sponsorships 136

Chapter Ten: Means of Blog monetization – Amazon affiliate program 140

Chapter Eleven: Means of Blog monetization – Digital products (eBooks) 153

Conclusion 165

Introduction

Over the past couple of years, the world has recorded tremendous growth – particularly in this and the preceding century. We've seen major technological advances – we've also witnessed a lot of paradigm shifts stemming from the many technological advances. There is no question that technology has changed the way we do most things. The way we interact, sleep, fly, etc. has been changed. One place where technology has changed the way we function is how we connect with each other.

Before the internet came into being, many people used to maintain diaries – these diaries were usually written on notepads or journals and stored safely to avoid loss or damage. With the advent of online storage media and the internet, though, people could now hold private diaries on the internet in the form of blogs. These internet-saved multimedia papers can be read on several occasions.

There is no single area of our lives that has not been impacted by technology. In the past, walking up to a lady in a conference and starting a discussion with her was inappropriate for a proper gentleman. A third party would have to present the couple (man and lady) to each other. Today, though, the opposite has become the case–with apps like Tinder, people can schedule a "meet n greet" or other dates by simply tapping a few buttons on their mobile device while sitting in their bedroom comfort.

Technology has also changed the way we make money–one would have to either get a job or start a business in the past centuries to make money. None of these choices were as straightforward as we just made it seem–you'd need to get a college degree to get a job, which costs a lot of money. You'd need to start competing for the few available jobs after graduating from college. On the other hand, to start a business, you would also need a lot of money.

Money making, however, has become much easier today–thanks to the internet, men, young and old alike, can now sit in the comfort of their living room, wearing nothing but shorts, and make as much money as they want. There are several online earning models available that can be leveraged by the average person to create a stable income stream for themselves. Blogging is one of those online business types. Hey, BLOGGING, you heard that right.

People often think that blogging is an obsolete way to make money on the internet–but nothing can be farther from the facts than that fact. Blogging has been a reliable way to make money online and will be a major online money spinner for those who know how to do it properly. The problem is that people are not willing to treat their blog like a business when it comes to making money from blogging. Note, something you're not concerned with is not going to pay you like a company.

We have always speculated to place things in the right light that real estate is no longer a viable company that can make you money. Moreover, when buying solely in real estate, there are still millions of people who make millions every day. There will always be naysayers and those willing to do the job–while the former group will be there giving reasons why it is not feasible; the latter group will smile every day at the office.

Initially, the name "blog" was derived from the word "weblog," which is a site and log mix. It is basically a log for faster and more secure access that is hosted on the network. The word log is a day-to-day record of events. Weblog was gradually shortened to blog. Initially, people used blogs as electronic diaries, where items that mattered to them were posted. You'd have people posting on their blogs about their lives, things happening in their homes, their travel experiences.

From what people used to maintain personal diaries, blogs gradually shifted to what can be used to communicate on general issues. Today we have blogs about politics, economy, relationships, faith, and so on. A lot has happened as blogs have moved from being just web diaries–people have found a way to monetize their sites. People have been making tons of money off various types of blogging since the early 2000s, and that will only continue because people will continue to seek knowledge, facts, and even entertainment until the end of time.

Although blog posts used to concentrate on the founders, today, you can start a blog and write about industry, politics, wildlife, travel, or many other topics that matter to you. That means that anyone today can start a blog, expand it, and start making money out of it. Starting a blog is no longer reserved exclusively for people like celebrities who have super exciting lives. Even if your life isn't as fun, on your blog, you will post lots of other items, monetize the content, and make money.

Blogging started as a hobby for some people, as mentioned earlier, but now you can build a blog and turn it into your own full-time business. We've seen a lot of young and old people do it–these people have done nothing spectacular; they've just treated their blog as a company, and it started to pay them like a business.

If you want to be one of those who currently earn blogging money, then you're in the right place as this definitive guide is for you. You may think blogging is saturated, but is there any company that isn't saturated in the world? Let's face it; any company you might think of is already crowded, and the work they go into differentiates those who make it in one business from those who make excuses.

The good thing about blogging is that it will pay you like a company if you put in the requisite time to handle it like a business. When you regard it as a sport, on the other hand, it will cost you like a hobby. That said, how are you creating a blog and turning it into your personal cash cow? What blog-style do you need to create? What are the common blogging niches at your disposal? At the end of the day, how do you run your blog like a real business to pay you like a business?

All these and more are what this both-encompassing guide will cover. When you dreamed of earning money by blogging online, take this trip. Even if you've been blogging for a while, but you haven't recorded any success, then it's obvious that you're doing something wrong, and we're going to expose you to the right strategies that you'll see your much-wanted breakthrough if you apply them.

Chapter One: Can I thrive as a blogger?

To begin with, someone operating a blog is considered a blogger–people often have this popular myth that all bloggers are great writers, socially aware, or intelligent young chapters that work extremely well with computers. This is nothing more than a myth–the fact is that anyone who uses a mobile as much as they can foray into blogging can be quite good at it.

People from all walks of life, ethnicity, sex, age, etc. have turned bloggers in the past few years, and that has changed their lives for good. One good thing about blogging is that it's huge–it's always blogging about something. You might be good at writing about dogs, cats, and other pets if you're not good at analyzing politics. You might be good at giving fashion tips if you're not good at explaining sports. You may be good at writing travel blog posts if you're not good at creating and sharing food recipes. Therefore, this simply means that as a blogger, you can do something –blogging is not reserved for a few selected people.

The only thing that can make things impossible for you as a blogger to flourish is a lack of passion, resolve, tenacity, and attention. It's vital that we note that while blogging isn't a get-rich-quick strategy, if you're doing it correctly, it has the capacity to make you wealthy, but you need to be willing to make an effort you need.

One error most bloggers make is that they believe they should build a blog today, monetize it tomorrow and start making money next week. Unfortunately, that's not how it operates–your blog is like your average company, you have to give it time, develop it until it becomes a money-making machine.

The mistake people make is that they want to view their blog as a hobby and want it to work as a company for them. When you consider what you do as a business, as mentioned earlier, it will pay you as a company, but if you view it as a hobby, it will compensate you as a hobby. While there are people blogging as a hobby, we focus on raising people who see blogging as a business in this book. Now, you need a certain level of commitment if you really want to operate a blog as a company.

Next, as if you were running a normal brick and mortar shop, you have to see it that way. Someone with a brick-and-mortar shop will wake up early in the morning; then, they will open their store. They take stock of available stock upon opening the store, then open their books for the day. As the day goes on, the store owner meets with clients, close purchases, then take more product at the end of the day, shut their book for the day, and go home.

Now, if a typical store owner does all that hard work, it means a blogger will also have some tasks to do. What some bloggers do not want to do, however, is the work aspect, but they want to reap the benefits. This is not unrelated to the fact that in the past, some revered gurus have given them a few false wishes. They've been advised you don't have to work online to make money.

And, the answer to the question, "is it really blogging for me? "That's Ok. You should blog as soon as you're ready to work. Even if you're not a blogger, you might be able to hire writers to do the blogging business aspect for you. It's also important to say that writing is just a small fraction of what bloggers do–the larger part of blogging includes generating traffic to your blog posts, social media marketing, and getting advertisers to advertise their products on your site so you can earn money. And, even if you're not a novelist, you can still be a blogger–just find a writer to build the articles for you.

You need to create a clear plan and concentrate on your goals in order to thrive as a blogger. You will turn your blog into a money-making machine in a short time with the right inspiration, commitment, perseverance, and a positive spirit.

Chapter Two: Starting a blog?

There are millions of 'make-money-online' strategies out there that exist, so why should anyone ignore many of them and promote blogging? This is a concern that would be raised by any logical person. Even if the other multiple online money-making strategies have the potential to make you rich, blogging is exceptional for so many purposes; then, we will soon be exploring these obvious benefits of blogging.

1. Blogging will make you rich

Though blogging isn't a fast scheme at getting rich, it has the potential to make you wealthy. The passive aspect of the income you earn from blogging is a good thing. It ensures you only have to do the job once and keep watching the money grow even during the days you plan not to work. You can have all the time in the world with such a passive income model to reconnect with your children, take a vacation, and do other things that matter to you.

Another thing that makes blogging an outstanding money-making business is that you can make money with your blog in many ways. You will offer ad space to marketers—with your blog; this is one of the most common ways to make money. You have a lot of choices when it comes to selling ad space. You can allow ad networks such as Facebook, Bing, etc. to place ads on your site and pay you on a commission basis, or you can create your own exclusive pricing model, negotiate directly with advertisers, make them pay you money to put their advertising on your blog.

You can also consider sponsored posts where companies pay you money to put ads on your blog for marketing purposes. That's how it works—a company is writing a publicity post that they can use to drive traffic to their own website. They then pay you money to publish the post and link it to their website on your blog. You can approve as many posts as you can in a month, and you receive based on how many posts you share on your blog. Remember, the only question in your possession is how much you can earn through this income model. Therefore, the greater the ability to negotiate, the more money you receive.

You can also advertise promotional deals on your blog and earn a fee when a deal takes place through the connect you've been promoting. Affiliate marketing is a highly profitable Internet-based way to make money. You don't need to develop a product with affiliate marketing—you are selling to your site readers the goods already produced by other businesses. If a sale is made through your ads, then an advertising fee is paid to you by the organization that has the commodity.

For both you, the company that owns the product you promote, and the customer, affiliate marketing is always a win-win. It's a win for you as you earn to promote the products of other people. It's a win for the organization that produced the associate company because other people are helping them market their goods and services. And it's a win for the consumer because you allow them to find goods that can help them solve their problems.

There are thousands of affiliate marketing networks with which you can collaborate and earn money by selling their goods on your blog. Clickbank.com is a popular affiliate marketing network where you can find millions of items to advertise and earn money from your customers. You can also consider joining the Amazon affiliate program where Amazon products are promoted on your blog so that Amazon pays you money when people buy those products or even other products through your efforts.

Many Internet service providers that you use their service as a blogger have affiliate programs that you can access and earn money by supporting your community with some resources. For example, to host a blog, you need a hosting service; you also need a domain name provider–both services are likely to have affiliate programs. Today, you earn money by supporting their affiliate deals and allowing people to purchase hosting service through your affiliate links.

You also need hundreds of other tools as a blogger, and most of them also have affiliate programs. For example, of email marketing purposes, you need an autoresponder, and most autoresponders have partner deals that you can promote. Besides the apps that you use, you should support a lot of partner software tools or products that your audience needs to think about.

Selling digital and physical products is another great way you can earn money with your blog. In reality, digital products are better because you don't have to maintain your inventory–you only produce a single copy of the product and sell it to millions of customers. The distinction between a physical and digital object is that, though you cannot do the same for a digital product, you can manipulate a physical product. On offline and online storage media, digital products are held intangibly. EBooks, software programs, and digital games are typical examples of digital products. External goods are some examples of wristwatches, suits, hoverboards, etc.

Now, before you can sell them on your blog, you don't need to be the developer of either physical or digital products. For example, if you want to start selling eBooks on your blog, you can hire a writer, give them a sketch and have them create a good eBook that you can host and sell on your blog. You should enter into a relationship with major brands as far as actual products are concerned so that you can sell their goods on your blog. Once you've grown the following of your blog, it won't be a problem to sell products to them, and the return may be quite amazing.

Through gated content, your blog can make you money—how this works—you create some special high-quality and high-demand content on your blog, then make it available only to those readers who pay on a subscription basis. You may create a site for members only and cover the more valuable content there—then when a member pays a stipulated subscription fee, you give them access to the only part of the gated page.

Though the above is not so popular, some bloggers are still earning money through it. Nevertheless, you need to have evolved the blog to a certain level before you attempt to integrate such a pattern into your site. Clearly, when you're just beginning, you can't adopt this style, and you've had to prove you know your onions as well. If you want the model to work for you, the free content will have to be extremely persuasive and filled with value to make the reader pay for more. If your general content is not sufficiently good, no reader would want to pay you money to read more of your material.

Some of the most popular ways to earn through your blog are the methods described above. Clearly, there are more ways to make money with your blog; we've just talked about the popular ones. You will research and develop additional ways to monetize your content based on your audience. We will conduct an in-depth analysis of each of these blog income models in a subsequent section of this book. Let's keep looking at the other benefits of running a blog for now.

2. Blogging will help you improve your writing and technical skills

Blogging gives you the opportunity to learn some critical skills, such as writing and other technical skills, and perfect them. Even if you don't write your own blog posts, you're always going to work with some professional resources, and the more you're working with these tools, the more you're practicing and developing. Blogging will certainly help you improve your writing skills if you're the one writing the blogs.

You're going to use plugins and templates as a blogger –you may also need to learn basic web design so you can always modify your blog without seeking the help of a professional who might be expensive. The more you're working with these online tools, the more technical skills you develop.

In fact, as a writer, a lot of search engine optimization, email marketing, and content marketing will always have to be done. Training and perfecting all of these skills will not only help you become a better author, but you can also use the expertise to operate your other online businesses.

3. Blogging will help you develop healthier habits

Besides helping you develop some valuable technical skills, blogging also helps you learn engagement and discipline art. Good habits such as self-discipline, professionalism, etc. that can be learned while blogging can be useful when coping with other facets of your personal and professional life. But blogging doesn't just put money alone in your pocket; it lets you grow some valuable skills and learn healthy habits.

4. Blogging helps you build a network

The first thing people do when facing a challenge is to turn to the internet to find a solution. You can attract people who will see you as their hero by owning a blog and posting useful content–these people will consume your content, post their own thoughts in commentary form, and some will even send you personal messages.

Some of your followers can go out with you and plan a formal meeting–all of this will expand the network beyond the imagination. Apart from your followers, through the useful content you make, certain marketers can get in contact with you and give you a bargain. In all, writing a blog can help you grow a long-term network of friends and associates.

5. Blogging encourages you to expand your understanding of things in your field and beyond.

There's a secret scholar in you, so blogging helps bring him out. As a writer, you need to study, collate, organize, and present information to your readers in an impartial manner. Also, because they see you as a voice in your field, your followers are reading your blog. Therefore, to make sure you post just quality content, you have to do the proper research. Your commitment would drive you to discover new things in your profession and beyond in your effort to put up new well-researched material on a regular basis.

6. Blogging gives you the perfect way to express your blog

No matter what kind of content you're sharing with it, it's still your personal space – so even if your blog is a niche, you can still intersect your views in your posts and make your voice heard. You can use your blog to express your views on fashion concerns while retaining a given niche. A blog is a perfect way to express yourself.

7. Blogging opens you to new opportunities and ideas

As an author, you can live on the internet practically–that ensures that you will always be open to multiple internet opportunities and ideas. It could be suggestions about how to make money or better ways to lead a healthier life–writing only leaves you more vulnerable on the streets than the average Joe. The more you become exposed, the better your approach to life. The people you meet will also have a positive impact on your life, and the fact that you have people who see you as a hero will make you want good behavior.

8. In the lives of people, you will make a difference

Thousands of people around the world are confronting one or the other problem, so they usually turn to the internet to find an answer. Such people are just looking for a little glimmer of hope or something to support them through their misery and despair. Your blog could be the tonic that somebody needs to get back their lives, even without your knowing it.

The above are just some of the few rewards of blogging–we'll talk about different blogging niches in the next parts of this guide and how to choose the one that's right for you.

Importance of Blogging and 10 Ways of Increasing Targeted Traffic

Have you ever questioned how a person manages to refresh his blog daily with fresh content without running out of ideas? Many blogs are going to leave you wondering how they manage to write material regularly. No one can doubt their ability to write prolifically.

Seth Godin, for example, regularly updates his site with fresh content. I felt I couldn't post when I was first drawn to blogging. But with practice, I now realize it's not impossible to comment. I've learned a lot from writing over the last three years. I wrote articles for various blogs and websites. Nonetheless, I still need to know more about writing to become a more prolific writer.

It's all about learning how to write to become a writer. Blogging is not challenging as some people might think. Below are four big blogs to show you how to blog and how to become a stronger blogger.

1.) Blogtyrant.com

2.) Copyblogger.com

3.) Problogger.net/blog

4.) Bloggingtips.com

Once you start a freelancing writing company, the Freelancefolder.com guide will support you immensely with guidance on how to go about your freelancing writing business.

A blog can now be produced by anyone who is computer literate. As there are blogging tools like WordPress and Empower Network that has streamlined blogging, you don't have to think about the technical aspects.

Importance of blogging

1.) Blogging is impressive: there's something you love to do (your passion). Go ahead and create a forum about your love and start writing. You'll know more about your hobby by writing. You're going to be surprised by people's attention.

2.) Proper use of free time: it's not a waste of time blogging. If it was a waste of time, at the moment, we couldn't have so many blogs. You should create a blog and start blogging instead of being idle during most of your free time. This will make you not ask yourself what to do to keep you busy whenever you have free time.

3.) Inspiring Others: Blogging has enabled people to encourage each other despite never meeting one another. People share and support each other's problems.

For starters, here's a quote I stumbled across that made me realize how blogging made it possible for an individual to get people's support, I had issues with depression and anxiety disorder, and it seemed like not writing about it created a false tale. As I expressed the problems I had, I was surprised not only by the support is given to me but also by the sheer number of people who agreed that they were dealing with the same issue."- Jenny Lawson

Yes, I expect more young people to start blogging and empower other young people who face different challenges such as starting a business, running a business, progressing profession, homelessness, how to tackle substance abuse, etc.

4.) Making Money Online: if you haven't found your dream job, consider blogging and earn some money online. Now there are many ways you can use to make money from your blog. By being employed as a blogger, you will start blogging for money. You can use your blog for advertising partnerships or using your blog to sell products directly to customers.

There are just a lot of opportunities to make money from a site online. It's up to you to decide how you're going to blog online to make money.

5.) Gaining recognition and drawing prospective employers: as a specialist in your profession, blogging reveals you. If you share information on your site and other blogs that require guest blogging, you will be known as an authority. Some people are going to seek advice while some are going to refer people to read your articles.

Blogging is also going to expose your ability, imagination, passion, and dedication. "Blogging is a great way to show potential employers your talents and interests while bringing a dimension to your curriculum vitae. When you blog regularly, it reveals your commitment, ambitions, and creativity— all of which are key attributes that employers look for in career applicants."-Lauren Conrad.

6.) Blogging improves your writing skills: over the experience, you become a better writer as you start blogging. You're going to learn how to express yourself better. Blogging strengthens writing skills and communication skills for others as well.

7.) Marketing and developing relationships with customers: in marketing, blogging is critical. A blog is a marketing tool, and marketers should use blogs to provide people with information about the products they sell. Marketers should blog details on the goods they sell so that people know how these items will be helpful to them in solving different problems. Blogging builds better customer-business relationships.

Big blogging obstacle

The biggest challenge confronting many site owners (bloggers) is insufficient focused traffic. A blog will never succeed without concentrated traffic. You shouldn't give up if you know that your blog doesn't generate sufficiently targeted traffic.

Because of disappointments, it is normal for anyone to feel discouraged, but giving up is not a solution. Giving up creates another problem of not seeking an effective solution. The most you can do is figure out how to push targeted traffic to your site instead of giving up.

Okay, why doesn't your blog get focused traffic? Some of the reasons are as follows:

1.) As it is still new, your blog is still unknown. This calls for publicity.

2.) Your blog doesn't have enough material to attract people and recommend your site for the search engines.

3.) The content on your website that you have written is not of high quality. The explanation of why it loses targeted traffic may be to post harmful content on your website.

4.) Your blog's niche might be the reason for the lack of targeted traffic. If your blog addresses an overly competitive market or one that people are not interested in, your blog won't attract any significant amount of targeted traffic.

5.) You haven't started selling a product that solves a specific problem, or you might be selling a product that isn't helpful.

6.) In search engines, you haven't configured your blog. You did not use the optimization techniques of the search engine to customize the site.

7.) You didn't build a chart, and that caused you to not keep in touch with people visiting your site.

They're never going to visit your site again because they're missing it.

8.) You didn't capture the attention of people. There's no material in your article that's interesting for people to learn. You haven't used stories to catch people's attention. You also haven't uploaded any videos or pictures catching the attention of people. You don't give a gift. People love to get free stuff!

9.) There's a number of spelling and grammar errors in your article. People won't want to go on reading a forum with entries that include several mistakes in spelling and grammar.

Chapter Three: Getting started

If you've agreed that blogging is something you'd like to do, welcome to this chapter, where we'll take you to the first stuff you need to do as a blogger.

Of starters, if you want to go to college, there are some very important things that you have to do before the others. Of starters, you must first agree on the course you want to take, consult with the admissions office, fill out some paperwork, compose a statement of purpose, etc. You must continue to accept the offer after you have been granted membership, make the necessary approvals, pay the fees needed, and then start your studies.

Just as nobody wakes up one day and begins attending college, so you shouldn't just wake up and start writing one morning. Blogging is, at least for now, a serious business, and it requires a lot of work from you. You need to consider how to blog, how to draw attention to blog articles, how to monetize your site, and how to can your blogging business.

First things first – choose a niche

Once people go to class, they just learn one course out of the school's millions. The reason is simple–you can't study all the courses offered by the University easily, you have to choose one, continue with it, and succeed at it. Even as you continue your studies, you have an additional mandate to specialize in a particular area of interest in your field.

Also, just as you can't review all of the university's classes, making a journal and blogging about all the random topics that come to your mind is not ideal for you. No, there must be order–people should know your blog for something that turns your blog into their go-to-place when they need that particular thing.

Of, cg, if you have an ear infection and you are attending the hospital of treatment, which of the following physicians would you prefer to take care of you?

Doctor A: a general practitioner who recognizes and manages all sorts of common ailments.

Doctor B: an ear, nose, and throat (ENT) physician who is a professional in curing ear, nose, and throat infections.

You should usually go to doctor B because he's a physician, and he's more likely to understand what's wrong with you.

You have to find a niche and stay with it if you really want to make money blogging. It may sound easy to find a blog spot, but it's not that straightforward. It's the first important step you need to take before all else. Even though in the future, you can always switch to another niche, it's better to get it right once.

The kind of community you want to attract should decide your blog niche. When you learn your target, writing blog posts, and other forms of items that meet their needs will be simpler for you. It's important to note that getting an established niche can help you stay centered so you don't write today about sports and write tomorrow about entertainment. It will also help you determine the best marketing strategies for you–this is because the kind of site you've received will have a significant impact on your blog profit prospects. That said, what's a niche?

What is a niche?

A niche has to do with preferences, programs, or items that only cater to a limited, targeted, or wider market or population segment. It can be said that it is also the smaller part of a larger whole.

You will find certain keywords in the above description that include "specialized" and "larger audience" or "people." Looking at the common uses of those terms, it will be easier for you to understand what a niche actually entails. The term "sport," for example, is broad and includes various forms of sporting events.

Today, when you're thinking about athletics, you're going to start having different types of soccer, hockey, cricket, and so on. In the broad category, all different types of sports are niches. You can still narrow down each specialization even within the niches—for example, you will include "international baseball league," and "professional baseball" within the football field, for example.

The niche is the overriding subject when it comes to blogging, where you concentrate on your site posts. It's more like the genre umbrella that holds and describes the content styles that you're going to publish on your blog. Sports, for example, is a fairly broad niche; you should narrow down and write about leagues in European soccer. You can further narrow down and write about the results of the European league.

Why do you need a spot for your blog?

Until continuing, this is an important question that we must address. Why do you need a spot for your blog? Of, eg, why can't you just blog on something as broad as soccer? Why can't you just blog about online gaining money? Why can't you blog about how delicious meals can be prepared?

For several factors, the blog needs to focus on a particular niche, and these explanations are not hard to guess—we've already identified some of them earlier. Imagine yourself in a large hall filled with people saying different things—they all want to be noticed in the building. Now, picture yourself in another small room where there are only five people—everyone in this little room wants to be heard as well. Which of these places do you think your voice is more likely to be heard?

Everyone will, of course, shout in the large hall, trying to get their voice heard, and this will make it extremely difficult for your own voice to make an impact because it will be buried in the midst of other voices. Nonetheless, you have a higher chance of getting your voice heard in the small room, as there are only five men. This is just the perfect explanation that the site deserves a focus.

If your blog addresses a wide audience, attracting attention to it will be tough for you. Even making money from affiliate sales will be challenging for you—this is not to say that your search engine rating would drop. Late starters in the game or the major fishes in the blogging ocean have already monopolized these large niches. You would find it extremely difficult to contend with all the existing blogs that already hit such large niches as a starting point.

It's also poor for communication to strike a general niche. You will most likely attract users who aren't quite involved in what you're doing when you write about a broad topic, and this will negatively affect user engagement on your site. Therefore, you need to identify your niche and stay with it from the very beginning. Of starters, instead of posting about ways to make money online, one of the choices or recommendations being offered is narrow down and post. There are many ways to make money online, and if you concentrate on one, greater traffic and contribution will be reported on your site.

You'll have a given audience with a niche blog; you'll realize what they really need and feed them accordingly. For starters, if you have a blog that deals on back pain, it's easy for people with back pain to respond to what you're doing and follow all your articles. Because you already know the kind of people you're dealing with, you're not going to waste time creating other posts that won't appeal to you.

Also, if you blog about a small audience, it's easy for you to really understand all the issues they face so you can speak directly to them. When your readers notice you're talking about the specific issues they face, they'll find it easier to trust you as a field authority.

Let's glance at some of the ways to find a great place for your site with that said.

How to find a blog niche?

You have two options when it comes to discovering a blog niche – go with the most famous niches everyone talks about or develop your own niche that applies to you. Some of the most common, in no particular order organized blog niches include:

- Technology
- DIY/Home Décor
- Beauty & Fashion
- Finance

- Self-Help
- Dating & Relationships
- Making Money Online
- Weight Loss
- Fitness
- Health

One issue with all the above common niches is that they are very large and that their competitive score is also high. The usual blog about these listed competitive niches when most people want to start a blog, so that's why they're really crowded. You'd hardly report progress should you start writing about any of the niches. Your blog would consider appearing on search engines hard —so you'll have to spend a lot of money on paid advertisements per view.

Instead of posting in any of the popular niches, you should take one of the niches, split it further down, and start to refine the scope until you find a niche within the niche that is still to be filled. For example, "car" is a large term—and you're going to get Mercedes Benz, Audi, BMW, and so on. Of starters, if you consider Mercedes Benz, which is a type of car, you'll figure out that you'll have Mercedes Benz S-Class Coupe, GLE Coupe, etc. even within that sub-niche. Of starters, whether you concentrate on GLE Coupe, you may still differentiate them by the model year. This is a perfect example of how a wide market can be broken down until it becomes very small and less profitable.

You have to take any of the lucrative niches when picking a blog niche and split it down until you get a really small sub-niche. This is called niching down in online business terms—because it's like climbing from the bottom of a tree and finding one of the many branches on the tree to sit on.

Here are the steps to find the perfect blog niche you need to take:

Step 1: Consider your interests

It sounds cliché, but you can't underestimate the value of posting in a niche that attracts you to be good at something like blogging. Note, you're trying to put yourself as an expert–and if you're knowledgeable in what you're writing about, you'll often go the extra mile to investigate and give valuable material to readers.

We all have different interests in life–some of us are interested in music, sports, business, and so on. You can turn that into your blog niche if you know how to make money online or how to fish. Look inside; one thing you need to be able to talk about very well, even without consulting a source— the next thing you need to do is to turn this interest into your blog niche.

First, open a text editor on your machine or open a new tab on your notepad, then write down the word, "blog niche ideas." Go to the next two lines and mention your writing interests or subjects. Such topics might include your preferences, hobbies, passions, etc. Make sure that you mention as many of them as you want.

Now, start listing more children's branches under each interest by thinking about specific topics or subtopics based on what you know best. This is one of the reasons that you are encouraged to go to a market that is of value to you, rather than one that you consider being competitive. You will be able to produce a lot of useful content if you choose a niche that is important to you, and this will increase your chances of succeeding as a new blogger.

In fact, uploading material will not be a challenge if you blog in a niche that concerns you. You will easily create new content that your users would continue to read–even if you don't publish every day, your followers will always be assured that the material will be of the highest quality if you write.

In fact, the readers want you to solve their problem, and how will you do that if you don't realize what kind of problems they have or if you don't know their situation? When you write about your interests and what you think, you'll quickly get in contact with your followers and speak to them directly.

So, once you've listed a passion, interest, or blog idea, and you've listed a lot of branches under each of the topics, add more child branches to the existing ones. You don't have to be a perfect expert on any of the branches of the child—at least you need to have some fair knowledge about them. Of example, if one of the broad topics you've picked is "baseball," and you know only some of the game's rules, then that's great because there are people who don't even know such rules and can consider your blog helpful.

For instance,

Let's assume that fishing is your broad topic; under that, ice fishing and fly fishing can be done. Today, fly fishing, as well as ice fishing, are both the major specialty divisions. Continue to narrow your search for each of these branches and find more branches for children. Of starters, you could have trout fishing, walleye fishing, and bass fishing if you concentrate on ice fishing. You might also have bass fishing and trout fishing under fly fishing. You might consider taking each branch of the child and niching down the more until you get to a narrower topic.

In the above case, the large subject of "fishing" has been narrowed down until we have children's divisions like "trout fishing." If you want to identify any of the categories or branches of children, you need to look at it and see if you can make it into an article. For, eg, if you've selected "bass fishing," can you build the content around that subject or niche worth a year? Once you opt for any sub-niche, this is a vital question you should ask yourself.

Step 2: Use a keyword planner to get more ideas

When you find it difficult to break your favorite niche or subject into sub-topics or sections for youngsters, then you can use Google Keyword Planner to get ideas. The Keyword Planner is owned by Google and included in its forum for ads. You need to sign in to your Google account or Gmail info in order to use the app. You can build one by visiting mail.google.com if you don't have a Google account.

If you type any specific keywords into the Keyword Planner, the tool returns a list of possible child branches of the subject. This allows you to get a clear idea of the sub-niches within the niche.

You just need to visit ads.google.com to use the Keyword Planner, use your Google account to sign in. Tap on "Resources," then "Keyword Planner" on the dashboard that welcomes you after logging in. Click on "Discover New Keywords" to perform new keyword analysis, then insert a seed target topic you want details about. See the photo below.

The findings you get from the analysis on keywords will look like the image below. In this case, "Ice fishing" has been used as the seed keyword.

Keyword (by relevance)	Vol (US)	CPC (US)	Comp (US)	Avg. monthly searches	Competition
ice fishing	22,200	$0.58	0.27	10K – 100K	Low
ice fishing gear	12,100	$0.75	1	10K – 100K	High
ice shanty	18,100	$0.54	0.69	10K – 100K	Medium
ice fishing house	3,600	$0.68	1	1K – 10K	High
ice fishing shanty	4,400	$0.40	1	1K – 10K	High
ice fishing shelter	2,900	$0.49	1	1K – 10K	High
ice fishing equipme...	1,000	$0.71	1	1K – 10K	High
ice fishing clothing	1,000	$0.76	1	1K – 10K	High
ice fishing jigs	2,400	$0.23	1	1K – 10K	High
ice fishing tent	3,600	$0.38	1	1K – 10K	High
ice fishing tackle	720	$0.37	1	100 – 1K	High

You may take any of the image's sub-niches and transform them into your blog niche. Once, you'll need to make sure the subject can be transformed into a comment. You can do this by making sure you can build blog posts around the topic worth a year.

You should bring into the device any niche concept you have and create as many sub-niches as you can. Once you're done, select one or two of the many ideas that you've got.

Step 3: Determine which niche is most profitable

You can choose a niche from the analysis and brainstorming you've done so far. However, before you settle for it, you can still do further research to find the profitability of any niche you want to select.

Keyword Everywhere is one tool that helps you search for the viability of a niche, subject, or keyword. You mount it on your Chrome or Firefox browser as a browser extension. What the extension does is to give you the number of people looking for that keyword or phrase in a month, whenever you do a Google search. Additionally, the method will inform you how much marketers can pay for the keyword or expression.

For starters, let's use a browser that has the Keyword Everywhere extension enabled to check for "walleye fishing" on Google. See the screenshot below for the search result.

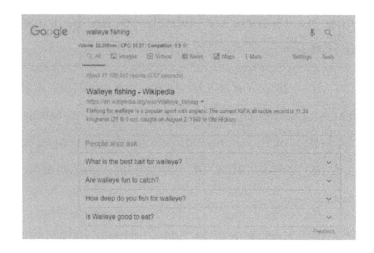

In the screenshot, you can see that in a month, 22,200 people are searching for Walleye fishing, and CPC, which is the $0.37 rate marketers are willing to pay for the keyword. There is also a positive ranking of 0.3 for the keyword.

Then, what you need to do is to add Keyword Everywhere extension on your computer and type in Search all of your picked niche blog ideas. Select the search button and record in a spreadsheet or Word document the figures generated by the extension.

See the screenshot below.

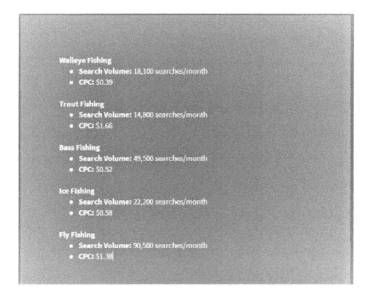

For each niche concept we use for this illustration, we reported the search volume and CPC in the above text.

First, you need to analyze the success of the niche idea overtime after calculating the number of people looking for each blog niche idea and the keyword's CPC. If a subject has gained popularity over the past couple of months, then you don't want to build a blog about that issue because it will quickly fade away the way it unexpectedly gained popularity. You don't want to build a blog about an already dying subject, too. The best bet is to choose a market that for many years has consistently maintained its success.

Google Trends is the best tool to measure the success of a blog niche subject or concept–it's Google's method. Use trends.google.com to use the app, insert a keyword of interest, and see how the keyword has done over the months in terms of popularity.

The screenshot illustrates the "walleye fishing" phenomenon.

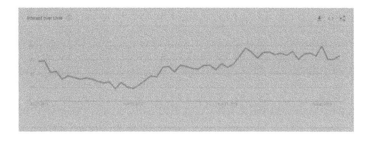

In the screenshot above, you can see that the keyword's usage fell during November 2018. Ideally, you wouldn't want to pick a market that doesn't draw regular traffic all year round. However, you can start your research and find certain keywords or related issues relatively popular throughout a normal year's seasons.

Anyway, put the other subject ideas you've received into Google Trends and see how they've stayed famous throughout the year. Since we use different types of fishing for this illustration, we may need to check for "ice fishing." Ice fishing may usually become more common around the winter months, so you may need to look for other subject ideas. You will continue to search before you discover a specific subject or concept that dominates throughout the year or for most of the year.

You should be left with just a couple of suggestions after you've sifted out some subject information. You still have to test the remaining ones for social media popularity, and you can use Buzzsumo to do that. Buzzsumo is a resource that tells you how much engagement a particular topic or keyword reports on different social media sites (likes, comments, etc.).

To check a keyword on Buzzsumo, visit the website, then type the keyword or specialty subject in the search bar, then click "Go." The website lists current social network discussions that include the theme or keyword that you have just joined. Throughout fact, on each social media platform, the app can inform you how many views, mentions, feedback the keyword has got. The product of the restoration of the website will look like the screenshot below.

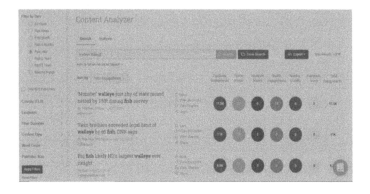

Now, head back to your table where you've reported and niche issue and the knowledge you've gathered about it. First, include the success of each of the market concepts (on Google Trends and Buzzsumo).

Check the niche idea's selling potential

You should be getting close to having a certain niche subject or concept at this stage that is most feasible among the different options you have. The next thing you need to do on platforms such as Amazon and Udemy is to check the sales potential of the niche topic.

The rationale for researching on Amazon is that eBooks are among the most popular products created by bloggers. Therefore, if you already have eBooks in your chosen niche that sell well on Amazon, the niche subject has a high sales opportunity.

So, head on to Amazon, go to the eBook category, in the search box, type your preferred niche topic or idea. Sort your search by indicating that the books with the most reviews should appear first. Note the number of reviews that the first two books that show up in the results have. Repeat this process for all your niche ideas – then sieve out the niche ideas that have books with a few reviews.

Check for rivalry

The last item you need to check is the page authority and domain authority of the blogs that already reside in the niche until you decide for a particular niche. A quick way to do this is to create a free account on moz.com and install the browser extension for MozBar. The extension to MozBar works like Everywhere Keyword.

Search on Google for each of your niche topics; the MozBar extension returns the page authority and domain authority of each of the sites that appear in the search results for Google. We are not involved in the authority of the page; we just want to find the authority of the domain of each of the domains that appear in the search results. If a website's domain authority is strong, you will find it difficult to deal with such a website.

Record the domain authority of the first website or blog that appears in the search result for each niche topic that you search on Google. The statistics must be rounded to the nearest whole digit. If a YouTube video is the first outcome of a hunt for any obscure product, miss it for the next link or page.

The table you use to report the estimates or findings by this point will look like the screenshot below:

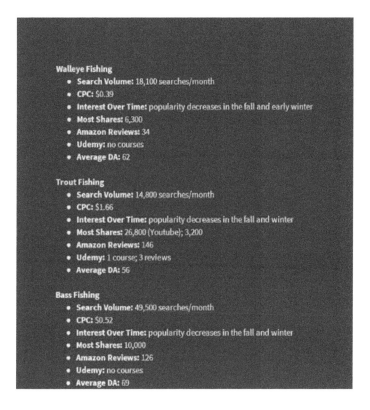

Looking at the above screenshot, you will find out that the highest search volume is "fly fishing" and "bass fishing." However, for the websites already available in the different niches, the domain authority is quite high. If you create a blog in such niches, it will be difficult to outcompete the blogs or websites that are already available.

"Trout fishing," as shown in the screenshot, has a small search volume, but the pages already accessible in the niche have an overall domain authority of 56, which is all right. Interestingly, the niche subject CPC is even stronger than that of "Bass Fishing" and "Walleye Fishing." Therefore, if you want to pick one of the three niches shown in the screenshot above, you're best off sticking for "Trout Fishing" because your blog will have higher chances of ranking on Google if your blog about that niche.

See how much time and attention we have dedicated to exploring niches and how to choose one? The reason is simple—once you've got this blogging thing right, you can be confident you're halfway into becoming a good blogger. If, on the other hand, you fail to get this stage right, it means that before it even started, your blog had already started to fail.

Now that you've selected your blog niche choosing the best blogging platform is the next thing you need to do.

Chapter Four: which blogging platform to use?

Once you've selected your preferred niche, the next step is to select your preferred platform for blogging. WordPress and Blogger (owned by Google) are the two most popular blogging platforms. A blogging platform is simply a software that enables you to create, edit, update, delete, or manage your blog and posts in general.

Which of the better blogging platforms? This is a question people are asking all the time. At the moment, writers, web designers seem to have come to a consensus that for so many reasons, WordPress is stronger than Blogger. That's not suggesting the writer isn't as successful as that.

When described earlier, Google owns Blogger, and it's a perfect platform for people who want to post a basic blog that they can quickly access and modify. Once you have a Gmail or Google account, you can build a Blogger account, which is one of the managed resources of Google. The good thing about using the Blogger network is that you no longer have to spend money on hosting websites. Google will automatically host the created blog, free of charge.

You can also use a free subdomain offered by Google if you don't want to pay for a personalized domain (which is extremely unrecommended). Let's say that your blog's name is Car Racing; if there is no other blog on the Blogger network that carries the same title, you can choose carracing.blogspot.com as your domain name. The ".blogspot.com" suffix would immediately be added to Google's chosen blog name.

You will need to acquire a domain name if you want to delete the ".blogspot.com" extension from your URL, and link your site to your new domain name on the Blogger website. Your new domain name will become "carracing.com" if you do that successfully.

Note: Google is still going to host the site. Therefore, you bill for a domain name only.

After your domain name or site name has been sorted, you can pick any of the blogger templates, modify them however you wish, and then publish your first blog post. A theme reveals how your blog's different sections feel when displayed on your desktop and mobile. If you don't like any of the default blogger themes, you can either pay for a top blogger theme or download one of the many free blogger themes available on the internet.

Another thing that makes Blogger scared of many writers is that it only has minimal themes and plug-ins. The framework is not used by many bloggers—as a consequence, theme creators do not find it necessary to create as many themes for the application as possible.

Plug-ins encourage you to add some interesting features to a software's existing features. Normally most app plug-ins are created by a third party to improve performance or attach more features to existing software. There are some plug-ins that will enable you to distribute your content on your different social media accounts when you install them on your WordPress blog. Some plug-ins help you keep your blog's safe. Many plug-ins will help you improve your blog's search engine rating.

Blogger has a minimum number of plug-ins when it comes to plug-ins. Because most users don't use the Blogger site, software developers who create plug-ins are focusing their efforts on creating WordPress plug-ins rather than Blogger plug-ins.

With only a few accessible and bland themes, several blogs are dissecting the WordPress blogger framework. Besides the freedom to choose from a wide range of plug-ins and styles, there are several other reasons why people prefer WordPress over Blogger. Let's look at WordPress in detail, and some of the features that make it perfect.

What is WordPress

WordPress is a PHP (programming language) and MySQL (database management system) content management framework. Another thing that makes WordPress unique is that for added functionality, you can mount plug-ins. You can also make use of thousands of templates or themes available–all this makes creating or setting up a blog using WordPress very easy.

WordPress's ease of use is such that anyone can use it to send a text message to their mobile phone. All you need is to download and install the website host's content management system. Continue downloading and installing any of the WordPress themes available–download and install some essential plug-ins–tailor the theme to your taste and start uploading blog posts.

Because of its improved security infrastructure, several bloggers and website designers still favor WordPress. You can download and install plug-ins to help you secure your site from hackers and cyber-attacks if you need added security.

There are also plug-ins available to help you boost the blog's search engine rating. This is another important reason why so many WordPress blogs choose. As a blogger, optimizing the search engine is vital to you because if you write the world's best blog posts and people don't get to discover and read them, then you've just wasted your efforts.

SEO plug-ins that can be built on WordPress aid to improve the website's search engine rating so that when people search for content related to what you have on your blog, your links can appear in their search results.

For WordPress, whenever you need it, you will always get help. Of starters, if you're doing anything on your website and runs into a question or technical difficulty, you can easily search online and find solutions on any of the several WordPress forums that clutter cyberspace. You can also receive direct assistance from the support team at WordPress.

Now that you've made up your mind to buy a domain name and hosting service with WordPress—next line of action is a domain name.

Domain name

A domain name is like an internet blog's physical address—it's what people are going to use to find the blog on the internet. Www.yourblogname.com is an example of a domain name.

Most people think it's such an easy task to choose a domain; but, when you want to start on the journey, you can find out that it's not as easy as it seems. You can notice all the names you were thinking were removed.

Note, your domain name is as relevant as your blog posts–it's one of the first items a guest sees while reading your site. It also helps improve the blog's search engine rating. It also lets viewers get a clear picture of what the site is all about. If you choose a domain name that clearly does not express your blog's meaning, guests may be chased away.

Use the subject of your niche

Because you're launching a niche site, there's no better domain name than one featuring the keywords in your niche. For example, if you write about guitars, make sure that somewhere in your domain name, "guitars" appear. If visitors come across your domain name, they don't have to think twice before they know the blog is about guitars and related things.

Except when it is highly necessary, try to stay away from hyphenated domain names as much as possible. Adding a hyphen in your domain name can minimize its smoothness and can give tourists a big turn off. Often, make sure that the name is not repeated excessively. Once it begins to reach two terms, it gets lengthy. A domain name composed of three characters is already lengthy, and if you're going to go beyond that, it's a full sentence that you have.

You must also stop using your name as a domain name if you are not a blogger in the lifestyle. Even if you're a blogger in the lifestyle, distinguishing your identity from your company might still be important. In the past, several popular bloggers have come out to reconsider the practice, both lifestyle blogs and those in other niches that used their names as their domain names.

Neil Patel, a successful blogger and internet marketer, once said he wouldn't use his name as his domain name if he were to start all over. And, even if you're a lifestyle writer, think twice before you use your name as your domain name.

A.com domain is better

The average blog reader already assumes that each website on the internet has an extension of the.com domain. So when you want to enter a website's URL, at the top, you include.com. If your blog uses a different extension, you may lose users due to the fact that if your future user adds the incorrect domain extension to your domain name, they will be routed to a different website and may not even access the domain name they wrote.

As bloggers look for a domain name, they usually find out that all the names they were carrying were all claimed. So, as a way to preserve the name they love, they often choose a different extension. It's safer for you to still pursue the.com extension some other variants of your domain name instead of opting for another extension. While some blogs do well with a.net extension, for example, the best bet is still an extension of.com.

Namecheap.com, godaddy.com, namesilo.com, etc. are famous websites where you can purchase a domain name.

The next move is to buy a hosting kit after choosing a domain name, install WordPress, download a theme, add the appropriate plug-ins, and start customizing your site.

Buy a hosting package

We mentioned earlier that your domain name is identical to the P.O. Your blog's enclosure. Your web host is now like the jar that holds your blog's content. Let's use a quick analogy to understand the difference between your web host and your domain name.

Suppose your blog is your parked car in your driveway. If someone wants to find your auto, they have to come to your physical address (your domain name) and enter your car (blog) within your garage (web host).

Various web hosting companies charge you various amounts to host your site on their website. Siteground is one of the largest suppliers of web hosting facilities. They have a dedicated WordPress website hosting service. Depending on your unique needs, you can buy a package for as little as $3.95 a month—the number of visitors that you expect in a month and the amount of storage space you need. You can go for a cheaper hosting service when you're just beginning and change plans when your blog starts to grow, and your traffic is growing.

It's time to install WordPress after securing your hosting account and get into the proper blogging business.

Since this book is not about the development of WordPress, we are not going to devote a lot of time to set up WordPress blogs. Several guides can be found on this topic—we want to focus on blogging for profit. Your website support section will contain instructions on how to install WordPress.

Upon downloading WordPress; then, a theme that appeals to you must be downloaded and activated. On ThemeForest, you can find incredible premium WordPress themes. While there are free themes that can still function almost like the paid themes, the fact remains that for several purposes, the premium themes are stronger.

They give a more professional look to your blog and give you more options for design. Note, your blog is like a company–you have to spend money on it the same way you'd spend on your business if you want it to compensate you like a business. Upon downloading your new theme, it's time to set up your blog.

As mentioned earlier, this is not a book on the development of WordPress, so we're not going to dwell much on installing and configuring WordPress. Nonetheless, there are a few guidelines you need to adopt while developing your blog to enhance your professional look, and some of these tips are listed below.

Font style and size

You need to choose a color and design that will always conform to the Internet-enabled device's ever-changing resolution. Tacky and childish fonts for your guests can be a huge turn-off.

Simple Google Fonts is a WordPress plugin that allows you to change font type and scale in various blog parts–consider installing the update on your

WordPress blog. The app often enables hundreds of different font types to be reached.

Color scheme

From the get-go, make sure you agree on the color scheme you want for your blog, and you have to adhere to this color scheme throughout. Of starters, if you've selected blue, white, and black as your favorite color, you'll need to make sure you don't use any other colors in any part of your site.

Note, the color scheme of your blog is part of your identity – it's what sets your blog apart from the thousands of others out there. It must be special, so it must be one of the colors used in the emblem as well.

Make sure that when selecting a color scheme, it is one that responds to your audience's visual senses. Science has shown that color influences an individual physiologically and psychologically. Many colors may affect a person's nervous system as a result of different hormone releases and cause a change in their emotional state. The potential inherent in colors has long been harnessed by marketers and business developers to influence the perception of buying and excite people's emotions.

Your site specialization will go a long way to help decide your blog's best color scheme. Mainly black colors go well with every niche or style, while mostly blue colors are used for blogs that are more oriented for career advice and related topics.

White color depicts innocence, simplicity, and intent consistency, while green literally depicts nature. Pink color reveals sensuality, femininity, and passion–for blogs thinking about marriages and heart issues, it's an excellent choice.

You will express your style, philosophy, and essentially your blog niche in any color you want to use for your blog. A smart way to find the blog's best color scheme is to check the same area for other blogs and see what sorts of colors they use. Do not clone the term as you would still want to retain the originality. If you glance at other people's color schemes, change them a little and come up with a unique scheme of your own.

Logo

The blog is your company, and like any other business, you need to create a logo that acts as a promotional tool and recognition tool. Looking at the Apple logo, even without being instructed, you realize instinctively that Apple made the gadget bearing the logo–that's the branding strength.

As well as designing and staying with a given color scheme from the get-go is crucial, you also need to create a color scheme for your blog from the start. That emblem will be your favicon and will also feature on your products for marketing and non-marketing. Once your blog or other material is opened by users, your logo is one of the first items that attract their interest, so you need to spend time cultivating this important branding device.

You can find one common pattern if you analyze the logos of the world's largest companies–their logos are all plain. Take a cue from them and even develop a basic logo. You can use Adobe Illustrator or Photoshop to create your own logo.

Adobe requires you to use the app free of charge for a week, after which a monthly fee will be paid. You could use your blog's one-week trial period to create a logo. If you're not a graphic designer, though, you may consider hiring a contractor to take care of your work. In creative services such as Fiverr.com and Upwork.com, you can discover talented designers. Do not assume that your preferred color scheme should be in harmony with the color scheme of your brand when creating your logo.

Once you've finished creating your logo, customizing your logo, and making it all ready for the site, it's time to start posting and adding material to your page.

Chapter Five: Getting relevant content for your blog

The next thing you want to do is to pop up your blog with incisive posts after setting up your site and having all the requisite customizations. We mentioned earlier that finding the right blog niche is one of the most difficult tasks—now, when it comes to writing, another difficult task is to build and write interesting articles that your readers will enjoy.

The correct people can consider the blog with the right content—this will function slowly and help improve the blog's search engine rating. Once you've rated many of your articles on search engines, you've always come closer to running a successful site. That said, you need to spend a lot of time studying and producing valuable content—one that would fix your readers ' problems.

Your first post

It often appears to be a difficult task for a first-time blogger to write their first material. The explanation is not hard to guess–typically, the writer doesn't know how and where to find the best suggestions for the subject to share with their readers. Some other recent bloggers are going ahead to copy and post posts on other sites. That's a very wrong move because Google would see something like repeat and wouldn't rate the site with something like that. Google can also penalize the site by stealing material from other sites, which will make it difficult for it to be classified on the search engine.

Another error novice blogger creates is that they just duplicate blog posts, using essay rewriters or spinners or alter some of the article's famous words or phrases. This is what bloggers do because they believe they will trick Google into believing the content is original.

Google, though, still has a way to detect material that has been twisted using rewriters or encoding methods for the post. Google considers these posts as duplicate content, and you might be penalized if you have such duplicate content on your site.

Now, how do you find your first blog post topic ideas? There are several ways to find the right topic ideas for your blog posts—one of them is by listening to socially.

What's Social listening?

Social listening means actually scrutinizing social media users ' messages and gathering useful information that you can use to perform different acts. When you go to Quora, for example, you'll find people answering different questions—what you're doing is responding to socially.

Of starters, when you join a Facebook group, you'll find people talking about different things—that's a kind of social listening. You can now take advantage of social learning—all you need to do is be proactive rather than reactive. Instead of just listening to what people think on social media, encourage them to tell you the issue they want to fix.

For example, if you have a blog about Amazon Kindle Publishing and you're looking for a topic idea to publish on your blog, you might be able to visit Quora and ask a question like, "What are the big challenges you face as a Kindle Publisher?"What would you advise a new Kindle Publisher, you might ask, too?"You might also ask," What are the best keyword research tools for Amazon Kindle?"When you find out that many Quora users would be willing to answer your questions, you will be surprised. You can pick up some pieces of information from their answers that will help you create your first blog post.

Including Quora, this form of active social listening can also be achieved on Twitter. Check for communities linked to your site niche on Twitter. Enter these communities and pose the kind of questions you have had regarding Quora. You can find a lot of helpful answers–especially if you find yourself as someone who is willing to learn.

For example, if you ask a question about the best keyword research tools from Amazon Kindle, you're likely to get responses like keyword.io,

Rocket Publisher, etc. You can now go to your notepad or word file to use such details and create an article such as "How to identify popular keywords for Amazon Kindle use keyword.io."

Also, if you ask a question like, "What are your challenges when running Facebook ads? "You're likely to get answers like,' My big challenge when I run Facebook ads is how to target the right audience.' With that answer, you can start creating a topic that says,' How to target the right audience when running Facebook ads.' In the examples above, you can see that your conversations with your target audience have already revealed the types of issues they have. You don't have to build patterns arbitrarily with such knowledge on your hands.

While the above approach is ideal for the exploration of ideas for blog post topics, you do not need to focus on it alone. Once you've got an idea for a subject, you still need to do keyword research to make sure the issue you want to tackle isn't a solo problem. Research on the right keyword will show you how many people are looking for a solution to the same problem. When you find that many people are actually looking for the subject following keyword analysis, then you can go ahead and create a blog post about that issue.

Keyword analysis

As described above, keyword research is an important step that you need to take while designing your blog material. One error that many bloggers commit is that instead of remembering their audience, they write blog posts about themselves. For starters, certain bloggers are just talking about a subject they're interested in, or one they think their readers will enjoy, and then they're writing a blog post on such topics. What these authors sometimes think is that they don't read their own site.

You're writing for an audience, and the things the readers would like to hear may not be the same subject you like. Because you don't just compose about yourself—you can be sure enough people are searching for the answer you want to provide.

Proper keyword analysis protects you against blind writing – it tells you the estimated number of people looking for a subject. It also indicates how much marketers are prepared to pay for a single keyword. All these pieces of information will help you find out if it's worth spending some time writing a blog post on a particular topic.

It may sound confusing to the new blogger when we talk about CPC (Cost per Click) or how much advertisers will pay for a keyword. Let's try to explain it, though.

Google and other advertising networks have a way to determine how much you receive by placing ads on your site or web page. One of the earning models is CPC, and CPM (Cost per Impression) is also available. Let's go on to clarify how all of this functions.

Three people are always concerned when it comes to the ads that Google or other advertising networks put on a website. First group, you are the user of the blog or website. Google or any other ad network such as Bing is the second party, while the third party is a business owner who wishes to promote their business on related websites or forums.

A business owner typically runs an advertising campaign called Google Advertising on Google's advertising network. The business owner discusses how much they are willing to pay each time anyone clicks on their ads before setting up the campaign. Many high-end companies offer higher deals than others, while some businesses offer lower prices.

Today, Google is promoting the company on your site or web page once the advertisement has been set up. Suppose the company agrees to pay $1.5 for each button. Note, Google has identified certain keywords important to the company (running the ad) on your blog for the ad to appear on your web. Therefore, for the keywords that triggered the ads, we may assume the CPC is $1.5. The business owner operating the ad must compensate Google $1.5 per time a guest to your site clicks on the ad; they will take their cut and give you the remainder.

Many keywords that are correlated with some high-end companies typically have higher CPCs than others. So you should be interested in finding out the search volume for the keyword and the CPC when you're doing keyword analysis. If the search volume is small, that implies that every month the keyword can draw a high traffic load to your site. Also, if the CPC is high, it means you can earn a substantial amount of money with just a few ad clicks.

The measure that you should check for when conducting keyword analysis is the keyword's competitive ranking. For example, if the competitive score is 1, it means the keyword is highly competitive, and for such keywords, you may find it difficult to rank. If the competitive score is below 1, however, this means that you can easily rank for the keyword.

Keyword research tools

We listed some of the keyword research's value - let's go on to speak about some of the better keyword research tools for bloggers.

1. Soovle

Soovle is a powerful keyword research tool, sampling the different internet search engines and displaying you the search volume and CPC of any keyword you use. It also tells you various keyword combinations and how users use keywords while browsing on different search engines.

What's more than that? Soovle is completely free – it actually works as a search engine. Only click soovle.com in your web browser to use the app. Enter the keyword you want to investigate into the search bar on the home page. Soovle will scrap the web in real-time as you type the keyword and will show you the CPC and search volume of the keyword. Instead, if you're concentrating on rating Google's keyword, you'll need to concentrate on the findings of Google. You will need to concentrate on Bing tests if you want to rate the keyword on Bing.

Besides showing how many people on conventional search engines such as Google, Bing, Yahoo, and YouTube are searching for a particular keyword, Soovle also shows you how your keyword is going on Amazon.com.

While Soovle is a great keyword research tool, it doesn't show you all the information you need, like its competitive score, about a keyword. If you need some pieces of information that Soovle can't show you about a keyword, then you can use any of the other keyword research tools that we're going to talk about in this segment.

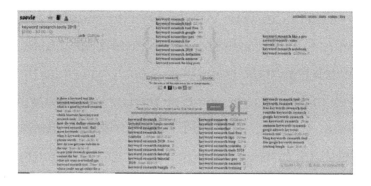

2. Jaaxy.com

This is another excellent research resource for keywords. Jaaxy is a freemium product, so you can use the free version with minimal options, so if you want all the apps, you'll have to pay at least $50 a month.

Like the other keyword research tools, Jaaxy shows you how many people in a month are looking for a keyword. One of Jaaxy's great features that differentiates it from the other keyword research tools is its QSR (Quoted Search Result) feature—this basically shows you how many other blogs are trying to rank for each keyword. If this amount is typically high, it indicates that the keyword rivalry is strong. If the amount is small, though, it indicates that you can rate for that keyword on Google's first page or other search engines.

Keyword	Avg	Traffic	QSR	KQI	SEO
seo link building	961	164	365	Poor	12
backlink building	334	57	250		72
one way link building	56	10	216	Great	84
free link building tool	256	44	91	Great	96
affordable link building	213	37	278		54

3. Google Keyword Planner

We spoke about Google Keyword Planner in a previous section of this book. Essentially, the

Google-owned app provides you with specific keyword details, so you don't randomly construct blog posts.

You need to have a Google account to use the app, then go to ads.google.com. Sign in with your Google account. Tap on "Resources" on the home page, then tap on "Planning" on "Keyword Planner." First, click on "Discover New Keywords," then type the keyword in the search box in which you want information.

You should see the performance as the screenshot below.

Google Keyword Planner is more powerful than the previously mentioned keyword research tools. It gives you a lot of keyword information that can help you make an informed decision about whether or not to comment on the keyword. What's more than that? The app is totally free–you only need to have a Gmail account (which is also safe) to use it.

Some popular keyword research tools include:

• Keywordtool.io

• Keywords Everywhere –this is a web plugin that we have already spoken about in a previous section of this blog.

• Google Trends–in the previous section of this tutorial, we spoke about this resource

• SEMRush.com–a freemium platform that does a wonderful job of helping you identify relevant keywords

• KWFinder.com

In addition to these keyword research tools, plenty of other resources are accessible, both free and paid. Do your research and find out what's best for you?

Interpreting keyword research results

You would be shown the average number of people looking for that keyword in a month if you conduct research on a keyword. You'll also see how the keyword is competitive. One may usually think the best is a keyword with a large search volume–while to some degree this is accurate, these keywords are often highly competitive.

Low search volume, low to moderate rivalry, and low CPC are the perfect keywords. Nonetheless, it can be quite difficult to find a keyword that crosses all three boxes. One of the conditions is a good idea for you to negotiate.

You could go for a keyword, for example, of modest to average search volume, small rivalry, and strong CPC–yeah, you will find keywords like that. You'd like to use your flexibility to assess the criteria that you want to settle on. For example, if a keyword has a large search volume, small to moderate competition, and low CPC–even though the CPC is weak, you might consider going for the keyword because the high search volume would cover-up.

In fact, consider their long tails instead of opting for seed keywords. A keyword's long tail simply refers to the extended types that can be extracted from the root keyword. You will see a lot of derivatives from that root keyword every time you type a root or seed keyword into a keyword research tool–those derivatives are called keyword long tails variants.

The root keyword may not meet your criteria in most cases–it may have a high volume of search, and the competitive score would also be very high, so you don't want to use it. Nonetheless, you can consider feasible alternatives with an equally good amount of search volume and small rivalry if you look closely at the long tails of the root keyword. Instead of the seed or core keyword, you should go for some long-tail keywords.

Let's assume, if you're searching for "celery juice," you'll see "celery juice" as a different result in the results, and you'll also see "celery juice advantages" as one of the results that could have high search volume and low competition. Now, instead of just writing a "celery juice" blog post, a smart blogger would write about "celery juice benefits."

One good thing about using a keyword's long-tail variants is that you may end up rating the seed keyword as well as its long-tail version. If you write the post first, it lists for the keyword's long-tail version. Then it may be listed for the main seed keyword after a while – which indicates more visits to your site.

Now that you've mastered the art of identifying and evaluating strong keywords, the next chapter should teach you how an entertaining blog post can be published.

Chapter Six: Writing an intriguing blog post?

Once we teach you how to write a good blog post, let's discuss the elements of a blog post like this first. A blog post usually has three parts— the header or summary, the core, and the conclusion or calls for action. If you want to create a highly conversive and informative blog post, you need to consider what material will appear in each of these pages.

The header or introduction

As the name implies, the header of your blog post will announce the post's concept or subject. It should let the user know what the topic is all about–if appropriate, you can include explanations here.

Therefore, when reading the blog post to the end, the header should let the reader know what they will receive. It's important to use emotional triggers to hold the reader engaged and thinking that if they don't read to the end, they'd lose anything significant.

For example, if you write a blog post about the benefits of childproofing your home, you might start by defining what childproofing means in your home. You could proceed to let the reader know that they will also learn the top five ways to childproof their home in addition to learning the benefits of childproofing. You've piqued the attention of the public this way, and they'd like to read your post to the very end.

The body

The blog post's main body comes right after the header, and that's where you're bringing out the main argument. You may recommend addressing your points in the context of a listicle for ease of readability. Subheadings or translations should also be used to distinguish one main point from the other and render reading through your points simpler for the user.

You're not writing a blog post about yourself, as we've always repeated, but you're doing it for your followers. Therefore, you can deliver valuable information to your followers in a readable format so that they can know you've supported them in the end so they can keep reading your other articles for more details.

Summary and call to action

The final part of your article should be used to chip into some pieces of information that you did not cover in the post's main body. Don't start repeating all the points you've already dealt with in the post's body–that would be an unnecessary repetition. Include a call-to-action after reading the article to remind the user what to do next.

Call-to-action is an integral part of every blog post–your average reader may know what to do next after reading your post, but they are still waiting for you to tell them what to do. This is your opportunity to get them to take the action you want. You should have figured out the goal you want to achieve with the post before you even wrote a post. To achieve this goal, you need to use a call-to-action.

For starters, if you want the reader to respond, use a call-to-action to let them know. Read other related articles, access an eBook, or post your article if you want them to enter your email list, let them learn. When previously mentioned, don't presume the reader knows what to do next—they may learn, but they still want you to teach them. Upon reading your post, the regular reader will click away if you don't tell them what to do next.

SEO articles and blog posts

Search Engine Optimization simply involves making articles so that search engines like Google, Bing, etc. can quickly list them. Many posts are frequently referred to as SEO papers when it comes to SEO, while others are not. The main difference is that in strategic sections of the article such as header, body, and conclusion, SEO articles or blog posts contain relevant keywords.

When writing a blog post, it's important to optimize the ranking of search engines—this allows your ideal reader to find out and read the article. It's very important to optimize your posts for search engine ranking because your posts will be undiscoverable without it. What's the point of writing a blog post if your target audience doesn't discover and read it?

Make sure that you used any of the keyword research tools that we discussed in the previous section to analyze the keyword before writing a blog post. Write down at least three keywords after your analysis that you would include in various parts of your article. Ideally, use keywords in your blog post's description, header, core, and conclusion.

Make sure you don't store keywords in your blog post excessively as it might incur a fine. Keyword stuffing is also going to change the blog's natural flow and make it almost unreadable. Keyword stuffing is the act of including an excessive number of keywords in your blog post in various locations for clarification. Those who do keyword stuffing believe that to increase the rating is a smart way to add as many keywords as possible to their blogs.

Instead of raising the blog post's search engine rating, keyword stuffing usually works to decrease its readability and conversion rate. Instead of piling needless keywords in your blog post, take your take and learn the right way to include the right number of keywords in your blog post–this will help improve your article's readability and maximize your conversion rate.

Write an entertaining blog post

Not the most cautious person out there is an average internet user–they also have a short span of time. It ensures you have to keep them as interesting as possible if you want them to read your posts.

Here are a few approaches to compose an interesting blog post:

1. Write in a conversational style

You can concentrate on the person who is going to read the post when you are making a blog post–you can do that by writing in a conversational style.

Such writing style will increase your post commitment by up to 80%.

Think about it—a professor comes into a student-filled school, begins talking without even speaking to the pupils, what do you think the students would do? Many of them would fall asleep because of the dull aspect of the lesson. But if the instructor approaches the classroom and produces a dialogue where everyone in the class is participating and feeling within them, what do you think would happen? It would be a fun college.

The easiest way to write is to use "I" and "You" in your articles in a conversational style. Using these two phrases will personalize the messages to the public—the user may believe you're talking directly about them. It's also a great way to create conversation and inspire more followers to connect with your content.

You can say things like, "I'm happy you're reading this post," "thank you for being here," "I'm going to show you in this paragraph..."

Any reader who finds any of the above phrases would feel you are talking directly to them and would like to continue reading. Without writing in a conversational style, your post will sound like an academic thesis or research paper, and no one will love reading these kinds of materials unless it is extremely necessary.

2. Break down your content into many paragraphs

If people open the blog post and consider it to be a huge piece of paper, they will not hesitate to close the tab and go anywhere else. You need to divide the statements into columns, and there should be around four sentences or four lines in each article. Create a new one once an article starts to get big. Presenting the thoughts using a chart is also a good idea–this significantly improves readability.

3. Make sure you use subheadings

If your blog post is so lengthy, make sure you use subheadings to explain your main points. Even if the article isn't that big, subheadings can still be used. Subheadings help improve the post's readability as someone can only scroll through and catch your post's main points.

4. Throw in images to spice up things

If appropriate, add in related pictures to make the articles brighter and spice things up a bit. People also search for photos as people open a blog post—people want to draw conclusions from the pictures or use them to explain what the topic is all about. It's enough to hold your reader committed to your message, something as easy as a crisp, inviting photograph. Therefore, well-labeled photos help optimize the search engine.

You should obey the advice above and compose as many articles for your new blog as possible until you've completely filled the page.

We're going to start looking into different ways to monetize your blog in the next segment.

Chapter Seven: what you need to know about SEO (Search Engine Optimization)

Search Engine Optimization (SEO) includes the creation and alteration of your blog material to enable search engines to conveniently index and rate the site. If your blog is listed on search engines, that ensures that potential readers who are looking for keywords similar to those you have on your site can locate your blog and go on exploring and enjoying the material you have on it.

It's safe to say that when these people do online searches, SEO is a way to trick Google to show your blog or articles to potential readers. SEO is very important in the world of blogging and internet marketing as a whole, and SEO strategies are changing from time to time, so bloggers are always looking for new SEO strategies.

The regular blog user depends on Google to get them to the details they're searching for. You will have regular access to your site if your blog is listed on Google so that the typical blog user will locate it when browsing. If the search engines can't find your site, the traffic would fail. If you're operating a popular blog that everyone already recognizes, then SEO is your best hope for steady traffic.

Since SEO techniques require time to deliver performance, some people believe that SEO is no longer relevant—but the truth remains that SEO is as successful as ever. SEO is your only chance as a newbie blogger with little financial strength to manage social media and other forms of online ads. You have to do it correctly, though; otherwise, it's going to turn back and hurt your blog.

Some reckless SEO tactics could get your blog penalized by Google. Some other SEO approaches could contribute to your AdSense account being disabled—so while you're working on automating your blog search engine, you need to be sure you're taking the correct SEO strategies.

Google and the other search engines update their search algorithms every day—these improvements also come with a shift in SEO activities. In other words, SEO's world is ever-changing; what's in vogue today may get outdated at the next moment, and that's why SEO's topic is always on the lips of every blogger.

Several times, new bloggers raise certain SEO-related questions like, "What is SEO," "What are the strongest SEO tactics for blogs," "Where can one outsource SEO services? "In the midst of other issues. It can be very difficult to react to the issue of best SEO practices or blog techniques because, as we said earlier, SEO approaches are constantly changing.

Yet despite the constant shifts, SEO's basic principles stay the same. If we suggest that the fundamental fundamentals have stayed the same, we imply that although some tactics may have shifted, there are still essentially the same stuff in SEO. We're not going to teach you specific ways to do SEO in this segment—rather, we're going to focus on showing you the best current SEO techniques.

The strongest SEO is to stay focused on the visitors

The error most people make when it comes to SEO is constantly trying out different strategies. It has proven over the years that it is not the best approach to SEO. Instead of running around and testing different SEO strategies or methods, it would be better to concentrate on one basic concept, which states that the best SEO is the one focused on the person.

Saying that the best SEO is human-based SEO can shock many as they have long believed that the best strategies include contracting SEO services to SEO contractors or using automated software, binary code, or shortcuts. Although many of these strategies may have performed in vogue a few years ago, they are no longer likely to be considered the strongest SEO practices nowadays.

The best strategies in today's SEO sphere are to learn who the blog followers are, to communicate with them directly, and to help them solve their problems. Blog readers are people who are looking for solutions to their problems, and if you perceive it this way and give them an answer to their problem, then you have the best strategy for SEO.

The methodology used by search engines to rate websites may have been updated many times over the years, but one thing remains consistent, and that constant thing is that every search engine provides useful information that serves the needs of website visitors.

Today, we could speak more about demand for results, smartphone inquiries, and long voice-based search phrases, but one thing remains consistent–the visitor's needs need to be addressed. Therefore, as long as people read websites, there will always be a need for high-quality human-based SEO. The strongest SEO approach will always be to have tangible value and concentrate heavily on user experience.

Don't think too much of plugins, data, and code on the website as the real SEO. Sure, all of these that come into play in rating a site, but the most important thing you don't have to overlook is to provide the best user experience to the web tourist, so they don't find it hard to find the solution they're searching for on your page.

You will realize that not much can be achieved for you after modifications or outsourcing of SEO resources to renowned consultants. The most important thing is that you give the guests the real value and experience. You may be able to bring guests to your blog through shortcuts or contracting your SEO services, but these shortcuts will not interact on a personal level with these visitors. Remember that the people who access your page are genuine people who are looking for answers to their problems, and you need to treat them as real people.

SEO is complicated and yet so basic

The SEO world is constantly changing; it seems that everything is becoming increasingly complex. Long phrases in quest are the order of the day now. Longer posts are also becoming the norm, so search engines are not left out as sophisticated algorithms have been built to be able to process all the improvements that are taking place. Nonetheless, we may claim that things have not changed much in the face of all these shifts.

Search engines are still looking for websites and blogs that offer visitors interest. Therefore, Google wants you to do the right thing, and the right thing here is to give people everyday interest.

Users often want to ask if they can play the system and use coding or automated software to move their posts to the top of the results pages of the search engine. The reality is that they may have worked in the past with these software devices and protocols, but they are no longer working now. If your emphasis is only on bringing the blog up the result pages of the search engine, that simply means you've lost sight on the user, and if it's not about the tourist, it's not the strongest SEO.

Human-based SEO is about helping people solve their problems, and you need to realize that black hat strategies are not helping blog readers solve their issues. We help you get your blog to the top of the search page in the best possible way, but

Google has built a fast way to remove the websites and blogs that exploit their game.

The bottom line is you need to take some time to know more about SEO, particularly if you're new to it. Do not choose alternatives, do not care about formulas changing; just learn the basics. Try to understand why people are visiting and living on blogs, as it will help you achieve your goals.

The attention should always be on the guests, their particular problems, and how you can help them solve these issues. SEO techniques can shift, but the core principles of SEO stay the same –helping the guest.

Here are a few items to do to boost the rating in search engines:

1. Improve the speed of your site

The average blog reader only has a few seconds to wait until your blog is loaded. If your blog doesn't launch within those few seconds, then you'd have to abandon the user. Because Google and other search engines also place the website visitor's experience first, it ensures your search engine rating will be increased if your blog loads quickly enough.

2. Reduce bounce rate

Bounce rate and site pace go hand in hand – the reason is simple – if you load your blog gradually, the bounce rate will be big. Google would be forced to believe with a large bounce rate that your link does not have what the user is searching for, and that would have a negative impact on your rating.

Although site speed is not the only thing affecting your blog's bounce rate, it remains one of the main causes. Certain issues that may trigger the bounce rate to increase include a poorly designed blog. If your guests find it difficult to maneuver quickly through your site, they will be forced to leave, which will boost your bounce rate.

Always make sure that your blog posts provide meaning and provide an answer to the reader's question. Google and the other search engines today favor longer to shorter posts. This does not mean that to make up your post; you should use filler material. Alternatively, make sure that you address any aspect you need so the reader will agree, "Yeah, I have meaning."

In fact, if you don't compose in a conversational style, you may also be able to chase guests away, and this will impact the bounce rate. If you don't know how to make innovative use of calls-to-action, you might be able to increase the bounce rate of your blog. You will guide readers to other important and similar posts on your site with the right call-to-action. This way, instead of running off after reading the first paragraph, they could go on a reading spree.

As mentioned earlier, studying all of the world's SEO techniques and tactics these days won't help you. Sure, you still need to learn certain basic SEO tactics such as writing articles tailored by the search engine, but if your blog is ultimately listed and you don't attract readers, you may end up losing your rating.

So, making sure your blog provides meaning is more relevant. Start by increasing the pace of your website and providing useful information. If you do all that, the bounce rate will decrease, and Google will be forced to believe your blog is good, and your rating will increase.

Chapter Eight: Monetize your blog

If you have followed this guide faithfully, you need to identify a web niche at this stage, agree on the right blogging platform, build your blog, compose, and publish articles on your profile.

Now, if you've accomplished all that, the next thing you need to do is to monetize your site and make money out of your efforts. People used to start blogging in the past just to record their lives or just for the fun of it. Blogs are considered by people today as a viable online business that can give them money while doing the things they love.

We talked about some of the ways to monetize a blog in a previous section of this guide. We'll spend time talking about the Google AdSense program in this section, which is one of the most popular methods of blog monetization out there.

What's Google AdSense?

Google AdSense is one of the automated tools Google offers website owners and writers with the ability to place ads on their website and earn money by clicking on those ads.

How the program works is: an advertiser approaches Google, creates an ad campaign, and then Google searches for a website that is registered in the AdSense program and places the ads on the website. Google passes through each website and makes sure that the ads they put on it are relevant to website visitors.

Google also considers the type of content a website has when advertising is placed. If you run a travel blog, for example, most of the ads Google would push to your site would be travel-related ads. It could be a travel company's advertisements, airlines, flight agents, etc.

Google analyzes the click action to verify that it is valid when visitors come to your website and click on any of the Google ads placed on your website or blog in strategic sections. If Google confirms that the click action is legitimate, it will pay you the amount agreed with Google (CPC) by the advertiser. When, on the other side, Google detects the invalidity of a click operation on an ad put on your blog, this could result in your Google AdSense account being revoked.

Who can enter the Google AdSense platform free of charge?

Ideally, anyone with a blog or website (who has no adult content or encourages betting / gambling) should apply for the Google AdSense system and get accepted. Many citizens, though, do not get their application accepted for some purpose. You will find people complaining that their AdSense application has been declined if you visit online forums.

There are several explanations for why Google would reject the application to join the AdSense system. When registering for Google AdSense, there are a few items you need to put in place. On your first try, the proposal would be accepted with those things in place.

Why do many people prefer Google AdSense to other online ad networks?

Until we start talking about some of the items that you need to set up until registering for the Google AdSense service, let's briefly clarify why many people prefer AdSense. Once we start talking about some of the stuff that you need to set in effect once applying for Google AdSense, let's quickly clarify why many people prefer AdSense. People often ask, "Why do so many people prefer certain similar programs to Google AdSense?"

The response is – while there are other online ad networks out there, the fact remains that the most common is Google AdSense. Thanks to Google's success and its digital offerings, many companies automatically pitch their tent with Google when it comes to advertising on online platforms. Facebook is also charging more than many other ad networks. Some other ad networks, unlike Google, do not have a straightforward payment scheme that guarantees that you collect what you received as long as the click you obtained the money is real.

Now, let's go on thinking about how to get your first attempt with AdSense clearance. It is crucial that you get your AdSense application accepted on your first attempt because your odds of failing to secure the acceptance on your second attempt are high if you struggle the first time. Google places your domain name on a watch list (this is an unwritten rule or code) once you've tried the first time and failed. So, at your first try, you want to do everything you can to get approved.

Approval with Google AdSense is not as complicated as many people make it appear. The fact is, if you're taking all the guidelines and doing the right things, Google would have no choice but to accept the AdSense page. If you've been taking all the steps outlined in this book so far, you shouldn't have a problem getting the acceptance of AdSense.

That said, before applying for AdSense clearance, here are the items you need to place in order:

1. A good blog site

Whether you're using the Blogger software or WordPress, when it comes to AdSense clearance, it doesn't matter; Google is more worried about your website's features. The blog site has to be well built to attract visitors. Google takes the site visitor's experience seriously–they want to make sure that when they visit the blog visitor gets the best experience.

In terms of design, having a good theme can do a lot for your blog. With a paid style, you're better off than a free one. Professional themes have better features, and to appear as beautiful as possible, you should configure your page.

So one way for both your guests and Google to make your blog appealing is to increase its pace. Google opposes low-speed blogs–the reason is simple–low-speed means high bounce levels, and high bounce rates would not enable advertisements to be viewed, and if ads are not reached, both you and Google will not receive.

On the other side, if your site loads fast enough, the user would be happy to read as many articles as possible on your page. Users might be asked to click on advertisements when reading posts–so Google likes websites that load more easily.

Besides supporting the approval of AdSense, the speed of the website also affects SEO. In the past, Google ranked only blogs containing the keywords the reader is looking for. Today, however, when ranking blogs and websites, Google looks beyond keywords and considers other factors such as website speed.

So, even if, in terms of speed, you write the best search engine optimized articles, blog posts, and your blog crawls like a snail, it's hard to rank on Google's first page and the other search engines.

You need to make sure that you include simple navigation on your site as well as ensuring that your page loads fast. Google recommends certain blogs that have the correct website features–all this also comes down to giving the best experience to the user.

Usually, when filing for AdSense clearance, Google wants you to include an "About Page," "Chat Page," and a "Privacy Policy Section" on your site. It shouldn't be a huge task to add all these pages to your blog–you just need to create a new page, name it "About Us," for example, and include what the reader needs to know about you. Google wants you to view your blog as a company, which is why you are compelled to include an "About Us" page.

You should have basic information on how your blog readers can contact you on your "Contact Us" page. You can include your phone number, email, or contact form to get in touch with your blog readers. You should include it in this section if you have a physical address for your business; otherwise, only include your phone number and email.

The "Privacy Policy Section" is the one that Google considers most seriously–in addition if you don't have "About Us" and "Contact Us" pages, Google may still allow the domain, but if you don't have a "Privacy Policy" section, the acceptance chances are almost non-existent.

There are unique pieces of information that Google wants you to include as you build your privacy policy account. This Google article will show you the information you need to include. If you find it difficult to connect a privacy policy page together, then suggest using this generator of free privacy policy.

Therefore, a strong logo would help make the blog appear as professional as possible. In the previous parts of this document, we have already stated that. If you haven't yet got a logo, then seek to get one as it will improve your chances of having AdSense accepted.

2. Quality content

Besides having a decent website, Google requires quality content before accepting the AdSense submission. They want to make sure the material you place on your site is the ones that can fix the reader's problem. Google loves the reader's experience more than anything else, as mentioned earlier, and they want to guarantee that the user gets a pleasant experience at every level. Google, the internet company, recognizes that if the customer gets a good experience by reading a site, the consumer is more likely to click on advertisements.

So, you need to create useful, articulate, and original content to increase your chances of obtaining AdSense approval. You can't just throw some spam content that you copied from other websites and expect your application to be approved by Google. Note, Google puts an emphasis on user experience, and as spam content irritates the average user, Google would never accept any blog for AdSense that includes such material. Posting the blog's spam posts will also have a negative impact on your search engine rating–so you need to avoid it completely.

Google wants you to solve the problem people are facing–once they think that your blog solves problems, they'll recommend it for AdSense. How are you going to solve the problem for people? Via work on keywords. Take the time to write a first, concise post after doing keyword work that addresses the issue you've found. Make sure that you overlap the article with appropriate keywords to boost the performance of your search engine.

One error several young and even old bloggers commit is heading to eZinearticles.com, copying articles, and publishing the same on their site, instead asking for AdSense and requesting permission. Some even build and fill auto blogs with copied material and expect Google to support the monetization tool. If you do that, you should not be disappointed if your submission is turned down by Google. It's good to put yourself in your blog reader's role–if you were the one to read your own site, would you be happy to read some of the material that you put up there? You should be driven by your answer to that question.

Ideally, make sure you've posted up to 10 well-written articles before applying for AdSense approval. Every article should have a duration of up to 1,000 characters. Before writing the articles, make sure you do proper research on keywords.

Once you've reached the recommended 10, don't just jump in and apply for AdSense right away. You need to wait a while and encourage the posts to rate on the search engine–this will increase your blog traffic. Note: Until accepting AdSense for the site, Google often evaluates traffic coming to a forum.

Overall, you want to get AdSense approval:

• Make sure you've got a well-designed blog with all the pages you need.

• Make sure you're posting articles optimized for the original search engine.

Quick tip! If your blog is in one of those big, crowded niches like online money making, networking, SEO, etc. then you may find it difficult to get approval from AdSense. This is one of the reasons why when you locate a spot, you need to narrow down.

You also need to wait for an AdSense application for at least three months. If you're just making a blog today, fill it up with posts the next day and submit for AdSense the next week, the application would actually not be accepted. You also need a custom domain name in order to increase the likelihood of being accepted. Using a subdomain gives out a hint you're not worried about.

Applying for Google AdSense

Once you have all the requirements, the next step is to apply for Google AdSense and wait for your approval. If you have followed all of the above-mentioned tips, there is a high likelihood that your application will be approved in your first attempt.

Follow this link to register for Google AdSense. You will be required to provide your blog URL, your name, contact details, email address, telephone number, mailing address, and some other basic information.

Important: make sure that all the personal information you provide is right, and the mailing address is accurate. For verification purposes, a PIN will be sent to your mailing address, so if you type a wrong address, you may struggle to validate the password. You will also need to confirm your phone number—although these tests will not take place until later, you need to get it right from the start.

It's not hard to fill out the questionnaire–just obey the instructions–just provide basic information about you and your site. You'll spend just a couple of minutes filling out the forms.

Getting approved to place temporary ads

When the submission is posted, the Google AdSense staff must analyze it to see if your blog should be admitted into the AdSense system. Approval typically takes place within 24 to 48 hours of application. If you've followed all the steps and tips in this guide, you should be worried about getting approval.

If approved, you will receive an email from Google that you have passed the first stage of the process. The email will explain further the other processes that you will have to go through until you are fully verified. At this first point, what Google does is to briefly allow your blog to run ads, and you are asked to do an address verification after you earn a certain amount of money by clicking on it.

You'll be shown how to place ads on your site at this stage – you'll also be able to log in to your AdSense account and see how much you've received from clicking on the advertising you've displayed on your page.

From the moment you are allowed to temporarily place ads on your site, Google must track your actions and guarantee that you do not click on your own advertising, drive traffic to your blog since dubious sites, or use techniques to maximize clicks on your advertisement. You should be fine as long as you don't click on your advertisements, submit buddies to click on advertising or use tricks or bots to click on ads.

You can discover that Google puts AdSense codes that you can grab and paste on your site if you sign in to the AdSense dashboard. These codes will be shown as advertisements as viewers show them on their devices.

Put various AdSense codes on your blog's important pages so visitors can see and click on them to maximize their earnings. Note, however, that the average internet user likes seeing advertisements, so you should realize where you're putting ads–for them, you don't want to scare your followers.

You will add your AdSense codes on those blogs and increase your earnings if you have two or more blogs. For each new blog, you don't have to submit separately – you just need to create new ad units and color schemes for your various blogs. You are creating a new ad unit and color scheme because you want every blog or website's theme to suit the ad shown.

AdSense verification

You can start producing ad units, put ad codes on your site, and earn money from clicks until your AdSense application has been accepted. Google will need to check your physical address, bank account, phone number, and tax information once you reach a certain threshold. Google won't pay you what you earned from AdSense without checking these details.

Log in to your AdSense dashboard to start the verification process; you will see a click that asks you to start the verification process. Google will deliver a PIN to the physical address you received when you press the icon. Between seven to ten days, the mail will hit you. The mail you get will include your PIN for authentication. To complete the authentication of your username, you will need to sign in to your dashboard and enter the PIN you have obtained via mail.

The mail will look like the screenshot below.

Your Google AdSense Personal Identification Number (PIN)

Welcome to Google AdSense. To enable payment for your account, we kindly ask that you follow these 4 simple steps:

STEP 1: Log in to your AdSense account at www.google.com/adsense/ with the email address and password you used during the application process.
STEP 2: From the **Home** tab, click **Account settings** in the left navigation bar.
STEP 3: In the **Account Information** section, click on the "**verify address**" link.
STEP 4: Enter your PIN as it appears below and click **Submit PIN**.

Your PIN:

If you have additional questions, please visit the AdSense Help Center at www.google.com/adsense/support/as. Our payments guide can be found at www.google.com/adsense/payments.

Thanks,
The Google AdSense Team

You may need to check the bank account information apart from the PIN authentication, but this usually comes later. You will be required to fill in your tax information while reviewing your bank account information. One of the bank verification requirements is that the name with which you applied must be the same as the name of your bank account. The bank account name must be the same as your business entity because you filed with your business entity.

You will need to provide your bank account number and routing number if you want to be billed by ACH (which is your preferred option). Google must deposit and remove a small amount into the bank account. You will be asked to enter this small amount in your Google AdSense dashboard as part of the authentication. When you type the correct amount credited in your bank account, the audit of your bank account will be done. You can then begin paying on a monthly basis as soon as you meet the minimum withdrawal limit.

You would be told to do so if you did not check your phone as you filled out the form. Google can deliver a request to your phone number that you will insert in your app or give you an automated call with your authentication address. Once you've joined the code of authentication, you're free to go.

How to keep your AdSense account safe

The validation and monitoring of your AdSense account does not guarantee that the account cannot be disqualified later if you do not meet the terms and conditions of AdSense. Invalid clicks are a common factor that could lead to your account being blocked.

If you're not clicking on your ads and you're not recruiting people to click on the ads, you're safe. Also, you're also safe if you don't use bots or click farms to click on the ads. You are also free if you don't place the ad codes on pornography pages.

You can also terminate your account by posting copyrighted material on your blog. The copyrighted material owner might report your blog to Google, which could result in a ban on account.

One of the factors you need to escape an AdSense account ban is that you cannot put AdSense codes on all blogs and websites related to the blocked account once you've been suspended. Therefore, you will still not be able to generate ad codes and put them on your previous blogs even if you get a new AdSense account. You're going to have to start creating and developing a whole site from scratch—it can take a long time.

The best way to avoid ending your subscription is to thoroughly read the terms and conditions of AdSense—if you obey those rules, you'll have your entire account to yourself as long as you want.

How to make more with your advertisements

Some of the easy ways to earn more money from ads include:

- Look and build articles on high CPC keywords

- Check for large search volume keywords

Of course, while the latter two strategies will help you earn more from your site, there are ways to play around or be clever with your ads and maximize your earnings. For starters, to determine the best parts on your blog to place ads for optimum conversion, you can do manual checks and ad placements. When you place ads on some parts of your site, your readers might not be able to see them and click on them. In order to determine the strongest parts for ad clicks, you need to do an A / B split check.

You need to place ads in one segment or position on your site to do the correct A / B split check, and report the number of people clicking on the ad in a day or two. Place the ad codes on completely different pages of your site after a day or two and monitor their success over a day or two. Use your AdSense app to track how various positions and parts of your advertising were delivered.

Once the best places where your advertisements perform better have been decided, stick to putting your advertising in those areas. For a while, when placed on the sidebars, their ads convert better. For others, when positioned horizontally between two links, their advertising performs better. For some others, their advertisements are best at putting them in the center of a post material.

Determining your own ad conversion hotspot can allow you to run a successful A / B split check.

Can I use any forms of monetization than AdSense?

Clearly, there are plenty of other content monetization services such as AdSense that you can use on your site. If you want to use these other forms of monetization besides AdSense, then you need to be vigilant not to flood your site with loads of advertising that could cause your followers a bad experience.

While Google does not shy from using other forms of monetization in addition to AdSense, implementing a competitor monetization system before applying for AdSense can lead Google to not accept your application. There is no official word from Google that affirms this–but other bloggers ' reports have shown that Google only accepts AdSense blog accounts that already have other related monetization programs in place.

You can place ads from other networks alongside AdSense after your subscription has been accepted, but first, you need to understand the reader's interest and make sure you don't flood them with advertising. There is no official word from Google that affirms this—but other bloggers ' reports have shown that Google only accepts AdSense blog accounts that already have other related monetization programs in place.

You can place ads from other networks alongside AdSense after your subscription has been accepted, but first, you need to understand the reader's interest and make sure you don't flood them with advertising.

Note: Obviously, these other alternatives to AdSense are not as popular as AdSense. However, when it comes to reimbursement of the amount earned, some of them are not as straightforward as AdSense. However, although AdSense has a rigid approval process, some of the alternatives are even more restrictive. So it's even more challenging to get accepted in some of the services than going into AdSense.

That being said, here are some of AdSense's common alternatives:

• AdThrive – to be approved by AdThrive, you will need to have up to 100k page views all-time.

•Media Vine–this ad network needs you to have all-time views of up to 50k to access the platform.

• Ezoic

Note: many of these ad networks are still partnering with Google to deliver advertising on your site. But, in one way or another, most of them are already linked to Google. Most of them bill you per 1000 trips, unlike AdSense. With every 1,000 views your blog logs, they have a fixed amount they pay you. If you get a lot of traffic to your blog, you can earn more from these alternatives to AdSense than from AdSense itself.

The only drawback is that before you can submit, they need your blog to have a lot of traffic. One drawback is that some of them don't have a straightforward analytics system that allows you to monitor their blog ad results.

Including putting pay-per-click advertisements and other online forms of showing advertising on your site, you can also earn money from partner programs with your profile—Amazon affiliate program and many others are accessible to bloggers. In the following segment of this article, we will address the Amazon affiliate program.

We looked at blog monetization using AdSense in this segment. We have seen that one of the best ways to monetize your blog is to place AdSense ads on your site. We also saw that approving your AdSense account is not rocket science—if you follow the steps in this guide, your account will be approved in your first attempt.

We should look at other forms of blog monetization in the next chapter of this series.

Chapter Nine: Means of Blog monetization – Sponsorships

In addition to putting pay per click (PPC) advertisements on your site, you might also consider charging advertisers to publish their content on your blog–but you need to let your readers know that they are funded. This is one of the benefits of running a niche site–you can write sponsored posts for companies that sell blog-related items.

When you write about mobile devices, for example, telecommunications companies can pay you money to share phone feedback on your site. Based on how many weeks, days, or months you want the funded article to appear on your page, the sponsor must compensate. The amount you get paid also depends on your blog's traffic. Usually, you can charge more if you have huge traffic.

How are you going to find sponsors?

There are two ways to secure your blog's sponsorships—you can let the sponsors come to you, and you can get them proactive and pitch. While the previous method is appropriate, it means you'd leave your earning potential to chance. You basically take the bull by the horns with the latter approach and reach out to potential sponsors.

Yes, the internet has made the planet a very tiny village—today, enterprises recognize that inbound marketing strategies requiring the sharing of information for their company on as many platforms as possible are one of the strongest ways to attract clients. Then, you can find companies that are exploring the internet for where to post information regarding their company.

When your site starts to get a lot of traffic, you'll be surprised to find out how many businesses can ask you to write guest products for them. As described above, these corporations are searching for high-traffic blogs through the internet where they can promote their company.

If your blog catches a potential sponsor's interest, they'd get in touch with you and sign up for a guest posting deal. The company might sometimes invite you to post and pin an article they'd provide to you on your site at specific locations. Your sponsor arrangement will specify how many days, weeks, or months your guest post will appear on your blog.

While it's cool to expect companies to get in touch with you for funding, it's better to create an endorsed or guest post strategy. By creating a page or section on your blog, you can do this by detailing your criteria for accepting sponsored or guest posts. Make sure you build a navigation connection to this page or site, and the navigation link label will say something like, "We welcome guest posts." You could also develop a sidebar or banner with the tag, "click here to advertise on this blog." Businesses in your area who want to advertise on your blog by sponsored posts or guest posts can contact you, so you can discuss an arrangement.

If your blog has a lot of traffic, and you know how to close sales, you can rest assured that hosting guest posts or sponsored posts can provide you with steady revenue. When you operate a niche site, an organization eager to market similar products or services on your forum will always be accessible.

When posting guest or sponsored content, one important rule you must follow is to let the reader know that what you posted is sponsored content. If you pass the sponsored article off as organic content, you could be sued. Even if you're not upfront with your readers about such posts, Google could penalize your site.

Generally, sponsored posts are a great way to earn revenue on your site, but you need to be on top of such discussions with your followers. Not being upfront about this means you could mislead your audience, which could have serious consequences.

Chapter Ten: Means of Blog monetization – Amazon affiliate program

We discussed selling ad space as one of the ways to make money with your blog in the previous chapter. We may look at another form of blog monetization in this segment, which is affiliate marketing. There are many forms of affiliate marketing programs; we will concentrate on the marketing program of the Amazon affiliate. This is a form of a marketing affiliate program where you promote Amazon products on your blog so that you earn a commission when someone buys the product through your efforts. Before we go straight into the marketing of Amazon affiliates, let's first describe what marketing of affiliates is.

What is affiliate marketing?

Simply put, affiliate marketing is a business model that includes selling the goods of other individuals and receiving a profit. Essentially, what you do as an affiliate marketer is: you are searching for businesses with affiliate services, registering with them, marketing their goods, and you receive a fee if any purchases are produced through your activities.

You will be provided what is considered a referral connection to promote a product–this link is used to chart all the sales that occurred as a result of your marketing efforts. You can get an affiliation connection from the affiliate program running the company or service provider.

There are various types of affiliate programs–more and more companies today have accepted affiliate marketing as an effective way to promote and sell their products; therefore, several of them have their own affiliate programs.

An affiliate program is a structured program developed by corporations that encourage interested individuals to sell the company's products and receive a fee. When mentioned earlier, most typical companies that you use today and most service providers that you use as a blogger have their own affiliate programs. Therefore, if you can advertise these corporations' offerings to your blog followers, you will earn a commission.

With your site, affiliate marketing is an ideal way to earn revenue–affiliate marketing profit is passive. You also don't have to develop a product or build a business. Others have achieved that for you, all you need to do is market an existing product and receive a fee. The keyword here is "promoting," not "advertising." You're asking your audience simply about a product; then, it's up to them to decide whether to purchase or not.

For both you, the organization running the program, and the client, affiliate marketing is a win-win. It's a positive for you because in order to develop a product or service you don't have to burden yourself–you will support an existing product.

It's a plus for the affiliate program running the company because it's a cheaper way for them to market their products and services and gain new clients. Last but not least, it's a positive for the consumer as the products or services you connect to can actually solve their problems.

If you've created a massive audience of blog followers, then by selling promotional items to them, you need to make money from this market. There will always be an associated product or service that you can advertise to your followers irrespective of your blog niche. Of starters, if you write about fishing, you might be able to promote your readers with fishing gear such as rods, nets, etc. Ideally, anyone involved in fishing would also like to purchase fishing gear, and if they buy it through your referral channel, you're making money.

Affiliate marketing did not start today

Before understanding it, you may have been doing free affiliate marketing. If you ever went down the road to a new restaurant, you liked their food, so you spoke to your mate, asking, "Yeah, did you see that new restaurant? They make some nice delicacies. "That's some sort of affiliate marketing, but you haven't been compensated for by the eatery.

Because in the past you have probably done unpaid affiliate marketing, why not consider doing the paid one? It's as simple as joining an affiliate program, getting affiliate links, writing a few product stuff and publishing on a blog section, and earning a commission when one of your blog readers buys the product through your affiliate link.

Amazon affiliate system

As mentioned earlier, you will enter and make money from lots of affiliate programs. Amazon's affiliate program is one of the most common. Amazon partner network has been developed to help writers and website owners like you receive Amazon's discount on purchases.

Amazon is one of the leading e-commerce companies and sells on the web every day for millions of people. There are also billions of purchases on the web every day. Amazon has already developed a solid reputation, so it's not your job to convince the readers of Amazon's legitimacy–they're just thinking about their strong brand image.

Ok, how that would work is: you need to make a post on your site about a product or a book sold on Amazon, you can use a special partner connection that Amazon can send you to watch everyone who visits Amazon and buys from you. By doing so, anything the person buys on Amazon in a 24-hour span will potentially be referred back to you so you might receive a fee. The fee rate you earn ranges from 4% to 7% of the product's size.

Why beginners would follow the Amazon affiliate program

There are thousands of affiliate programs and affiliate marketing networks out there that you can continue with; but, beginners are often advised to start their affiliate marketing journey with Amazon affiliate program for so many reasons including the ones below:

1. It is easier

If you want to continue with the other affiliate marketing networks or services, you need strong sales management skills. By being a cold lead to a warm customer, you need to learn how to offer and take people.

You don't have to do that with Amazon.com affiliate program. Amazon is a global brand, and its website has been perfected to the extent that simply visiting the site brings people into a buying mode. It ensures there must be something for them to shop several times when people visit the website. Therefore, whenever they make a purchase, the only task is to drive traffic to the site and make money.

2. There are unlimited products to promote

There are unlimited products for promoting Amazon's products, and niches continue to grow daily. In fact, every single day, thousands of new products are added to the website. When one company or market is crowded, you will support and make money from thousands of new fast selling products. And you can always consider something that you can support relevant to your niche.

3. You can make money from the sales of products you didn't pitch

You will make a lot of money selling non-pitched goods. Let's assume, for starters, that your specialty is audio equipment. And you're testing then suggesting all sorts of microphones to users. That occurs is, if you refer someone to Amazon, and maybe the person gets to Amazon.com, changes his mind and decides to buy a television set instead, as long as the purchase was made within 24 hours from the date you referred the buyer to Amazon, you will still receive money, even if they did not purchase the original product you sold to them.

How to join

It is free to join the affiliate program of Amazon.com. You will see a button as you visit the website that states, "Join Now for Free," click on the button, fill out the form with the right information, and you're ready to go.

Obviously, you'd like to promote your blog, niche related products. For example, if your blog is about movies and music, along with visual equipment, you would like to support audio equipment, headphones, and other audio products.

Many blogs make the mistake of making a site in one niche when selling items in a specific niche. If you do that, you won't be taken seriously by your readers.

Consider that—if someone is still reading about a particular topic on your blog and they see a chance on Amazon to buy anything similar to that article, they'd take the opportunity. This is one explanation of why the affiliate program of Amazon.com is perfect for bloggers.

Many people who read niche blogs are often seekers of answers, so they would love it if you bring them to a product that would provide them with the answer they are searching for. For starters, if you write about how to make money online and advertise a book that teaches your followers how to set up autoresponders, they wouldn't hesitate to buy the book, thus helping you receive a fee from an affiliate.

How to extract your affiliate link?

You need to extract an affiliate link for that product and use the link when posting on your blog or sending marketing emails if you want to earn money from selling a product. It often seems difficult to get this affiliate connection for individual products, particularly for beginners. It's not that hard, though.

• Connect to your Amazon partner account is the first move.

• The second step is to look for the commodity you want to endorse

• Remove affiliate links from your partner.

Let's go into depth about these:

Once you've signed in to your Amazon affiliate program account, take a look at the top menu, and you'll see that next to the "Back" button, there's a

"Service Linking" link. Pick the very first alternative that says, "Brand Connect." Look further down the opening new page and see a search bar.

Now type the keyword you want to advertise for the company you like. For starters, if you want to endorse men's training boots, simply type in the search bar "training boots" and click "Go."

Hitting the "Go" button will show several search results relevant to the keywords that you entered. You will see an orange button next to each search result that will provide a referral connection for that particular product. Click the arrow next to where it says, "Get link;" you will receive a pop-up box with an affiliate link to the product when you click on it.

You will find, on close observation, that the connection does not really look nice, and if you use the link as it is on your page, it could be misconstrued as a spam link.

How are you going to solve this puzzle? You'll see two buttons on top of the box that pops up.

Another suggests, "Copy and paste the link below," while the other notes, "shorten connection to amazon.to." Then, press the second button, and the partner link will be simplified to something more convenient and simpler. Certain connection shortening tools are also available that can fulfill a similar purpose, such as bit.ly, etc. Now include in your product reviews the connection thus received, YouTube overview boxes, social media posts, or any other location where you plan to generate traffic for your affiliate products. For all the goods you want to endorse, repeat this process.

How to compose a sales article for an affiliate company?

When it comes to Amazon affiliate marketing, you need to actively promote the affiliate items on your site to make the readers understand the product's advantages and decide to buy.

You may consider writing a review post about the company for some items and then include the promotional connection of the product in the article. One major problem people face when creating promo content for affiliate items is that they don't know what to write, particularly if they haven't used that product.

If you want to get suggestions on what to post about a promotional company, the best bet is to check the Amazon platform, search for the product you want to advertise, browse at five of the latest reviews and see what consumers are talking about the product. Customer reviews are generally frank and will always show a product's positives, drawbacks. Now your job is to take all this information and compile it into an article and post on your blog that is very easy to read.

That's the interest you're going to give visitors to your blog. Include the promotional connection to the product at the end of the article or blog post and receive a fee any time anyone purchases the product through your page.

Joining the Amazon affiliate program is a great way to earn money on your site—you will support thousands of products. What's more than that? The earning potential is huge, and while you're sleeping, you might make some money.

Chapter Eleven: Means of Blog monetization – Digital products (eBooks)

Including selling ad space and participating in affiliate marketing, selling digital items such as eBooks and online courses is another way to earn money with your blog. In reality, eBooks are like hot cakes today–more and more people are looking for content every day, and if you bundle material people are looking for in the form of an eBook, the consumers would be happy to buy it.

As a niche writer, you get a perfect understanding of your market–you recognize the pain points or questions your followers might have. If you really paid attention to your audience, you would have deduced some of their major issues. You can find it difficult to aggregate all the things into a blog post several times, so you may need to compile it all into an eBook.

How do you get ideas on the subject of eBook?

The best way to get suggestions on eBook topics is to visit Amazon.com and then go to the segment on books / Kindle. Tap through the segment where you find your niche-related books. Look at the books that sell there already. Read the reviews left on the books and see what people are saying in the past who purchased the books. Take note of the negative reviews so that in your novel, you will fix them.

For example, a website like Amazon enables you to access the first few pages of a book sold on its site. You will leverage this function to look at some of the books published in your niche's table of contents. Use the details you get to build your eBook's table of contents.

You will start writing your eBook with the content table in your pocket. Make sure the eBook contains valuable information so your readers can say, "wow, I've learned a lot from this." If you don't have the time to sit down and write, or if you can't write long eBooks, you can hire ghostwriters on freelance platforms such as Fiverr.com and Upwork.com to help you write an eBook. You will typically need to provide an overview to the ghostwriter and negotiate with them certain eBook information.

It's time to start proactive eBook promotion after writing and publishing the eBook on sites, including Amazon.com and other self-publishing channels. To create awareness for the eBook, you should create a post on your site. You may sell your followers the eBook at a discount price–then invite them after reading the book to drop a comment. The reviews will help improve the book's ranking and make it read by other people as well.

Note, one book is not enough when it comes to making money with eBooks–you have to publish as many books as you can. You need to have at least five (5) books to continue seeing a reasonable income, and you need to sell them vigorously to your audience. Since each of the books is in your market, you need to connect them all together so that the majority of the books can be purchased from customers buying one.

Amazon takes some of the money for every transaction you make of your eBook and charges you the remainder after a certain time. If you want to stop Amazon getting this fee, then you might try storing the eBook on your website–selling it directly on your site. You need a payment processor such as PayPal or a vendor account to do this.

Send them a download link to their eBook once a customer purchases the eBook directly from your blog, and you confirm their payment. Convert the eBook into ePub, PDF, Mobi, or any of the other common eBook formats to make it accessible on many platforms. Selling your eBook directly on your website, you could never go wrong as you get to keep all the money.

You will build video courses and market them to your readers as well as selling eBooks. Essentially, the procedure is the same as creating an eBook. You can post the video course on your site and market it to your followers, or you can host it on websites such as udemy.com Lynda.com, etc.

You might consider creating a members-only section on your blog if you don't want to create courses or eBooks. It section can include gated access or exclusive details that only those who pay a subscription fee will be made available.

You need to make sure that the general pages on your site provide valuable information to encourage people to join the members-only portion. This way, readers would look forward to seeing what's in the gated area. It's human nature basic—we're still intrigued or curious to know what's behind the curtain. Then, you need to manipulate and make money from this human nature.

Note, if people join your members-only segment and figure out there's any basic information they could want elsewhere, they'd quit, and that'd make the community unhappy. So, you should only create a members-only section if you have information that you don't think should be shared free of charge.

When you decide to create a section for members only, people might try to guilt-trip you into keeping it all free. Those are people who believe the knowledge should be worth zero. Whereas, for the same knowledge, those same people go to college and pay huge money. Essentially, if you have any interest, don't be afraid or guilty of handing it out free of charge.

Those who know the information's value will pay for having it. If anyone doubts the importance of information and the need to monetize it, that person is not your ideal customer anyway, and you should not worry about such people. You should be more interested in those who place a premium on valuable information and ensure that you give real value to them.

We have just summarized some passive revenue methods in this chapter that you can leverage and make money on your blog.

Email marketing to sell more

Anything you offer on your site, you need to create an email list— your email subscribers are like your loyal customers— you might advertise every product or service to them, and they'd purchase it. Money is often said in the online business scene in the chart, and that's real. When you learn how to maximize the collection, so selling anything, you can make money.

Why is the list of emails so important?

To explain why a list is relevant, let's examine how the market and selling landscape has evolved over the past few years. In the past, just to develop a good commodity, a corporation needed to send salespeople to sell the goods. Customers might buy any product these days as long as the seller who markets the product is reasonably persuasive.

Today, however, a lot has changed–the average customer now has a lot of choices to make. They're actually just a Google search away from finding the right products to solve their problems. How do you persuade the average customer to patronize you and abandon your rivals in an environment where thousands of other people market the same goods you sell or provide the same service you provide? The answer is simple–you have to connect emotionally with the client.

How do you communicate with the customer emotionally? Next, you have to recognize that the average customer buys on the basis of impulses nowadays, and objectively explains it. Therefore, to get them to purchase from you, you need to get them motivated and make them feel emotionally connected to both you and your company as a brand. The only way you can do this is to get in contact with them and connect with them as friends.

The propinquity impact can take its course as you continually interact with your clients, writers, or potential customers to make them want to patronize something you sell. You can connect with your community through emails apart from writing blog posts.

You will capture your readers' emails with the correct lead generation plan to make sure you send them the appropriate newsletters. You will transform your fans or subscribers into loyal customers with the right emails that will buy your products and keep reading your posts.

Because you already have a following, getting a blog allows email marketing too simple–you need to attract them with emails and warm them up about a company and sell the product to them. The first step in email marketing is typically to gain an immense audience that could be transmitted through an autoresponder.

Then the second stage is to use an autoresponder to warm up the broad audience and narrowly segment your list into those who may need your product right away and those who may need it later. Keep using a sequence of email swipes to warm up customers before eventually they are ready to purchase and then sell a commodity to them. Generally, this whole process takes time– from the first-day subscribers enter the list to the day they are ready to purchase. Research shows that a subscriber must be prepared to buy up to 7 contacts. This ensures that you have to send multiple reminders to your potential customers before they are actually ready to buy.

Let's get realistic

Let's say you've produced an eBook and use email marketing for advertising this eBook and selling it. Here's what you need to do:

1. Second, to enter the email list, you will use something to impress your potential customers. Remember, reading your blog posts by someone doesn't make the person your client. The user is just a potential customer at most, and you need to get them to access your email list so you can transform them into customers.

You need to use something to attract them to get your followers to access your email list. For starters, build and give your readers a free eBook lead magnet or tripwire. It might be a short reading to make them salivate and want more.

The lead magnet or tripwire must be very captivating so that after reading, the reader would ask for more. The free lead magnet is to allow the user to buy the paying eBook or leave their email to get more details about how to get the paid bid.

2. Make a post on your blog after you have developed the lead magnet and sell it to your followers. You can use other methods of lead generation (discussed in the chapter) to provide your readers with the lead magnet.

3. Using ClickFunnels or any of the other autoresponders such as MailChimp to build a landing page. Give them a "thank you" note and a click to access their free lead magnet once a prospective user sends their email to allow them to download the free eBook or bid.

4. Now that you've got their addresses use a set of well-crafted email swipes to remind them about the paying eBook you want them to purchase. Tell them the product's advantages and why they need to order it. Your arguments should be strong enough to make the purchase decision of the

customer. They could also include psychological data to further reassure prospective customers.

5. Please introduce them to the company you want to market to them once you have warmed up the leads for a while.

The above strategy works like a charm because even if customers don't buy the actual product you're selling to them, you still have their email, and you could later sell them more items.

Anything you offer on your site, email marketing is always going to be important, and if you know how to use it effectively, you're going to be miles ahead of your competition.

Conclusion

Blogging is stale!!!

I'm sure you've heard the above claim many times— those who jumped into blogging without proper research are usually saying it. Several people went on to comment and, after the first year, were unable to renew their domain name. These are the kinds of people that make the type of claim above; they did not do their due diligence until they went into blogging, as mentioned earlier.

I'm sure you've been convinced after reading this book that blogging isn't dead yet and won't die in the coming years. If there's an online business that's going to be successful for so long, it's blogging. People are known to be seekers of information, and blogging will continue to be important as long as people continue to seek knowledge every day.

Nonetheless, you need to be ready to work for you to do it as a writer. Don't be like those who see blogging as a side hustle when they're out of work they could fall back on. Although many people have claimed that blogging is a side job, in the real sense of the word, it is not really a side hustle.

Blogging is a full-time business, and if you don't treat it as a full-time business, it won't pay you like a business, and you'll probably end up joining those who say it's dead. How many hours do you think a good blogging niche will take you to research? It might take up to five days or even a week for you. Would you say that a side hustle is something that takes so much time to do?

You'll need to start designing your site when you've discovered a writing area. If you don't have the resources to hire a web designer, you'd have to personalize and create the site on your own. Again, it's going to take a long time. Would you call a side hustle something that demands so much time?

You will begin investigating keywords for blog posts or papers after creating and customizing your site. You will need to compose concise articles after rounds of keyword analysis, and they need to be tailored for the search engine. If they are not designed for keywords, they will not be indexed by Google and the other search engines, so the attempts will be in vain.

It can take you many hours to compose good and high blog posts, if not days –is that what you consider a side hustle? Blogging is not a side hustle, so it requires you to pay full attention to it. You'll transform your blog into a money-making machine in no time with determination, hard work, perseverance. Then all the work you placed into it will make sense for you.

Blogging is the form of online business used by other online companies. It ensures you can earn money by affiliate marketing, eBook purchases, and many other strategies apart from the standard AdSense system that everyone talks about. And if you've set up your blog to a certain level, you might be able to dive into those other online businesses full time.

So, as a blogger, your earning potential is just huge, and most earning methods are completely passive.

It ensures that while you're sleeping, you can make money. Affiliate marketing, for starters, is an ideal way to make money from your blog. And if you do well, loyalty ads will provide you with passive income.

Sales of EBooks is also another way to earn money from your blog, and if done properly, you will earn a lot of passive income by following the instructions in this text. If you add all the earning possibilities with a major such as AdSense, you consider it definitely worth writing. You just have to give it time and commitment, and to take care of you afterward, it will turn around.

You're going to have to work your ass off at first— you're going to have to devote time to the blog. But the site will be able to stand alone as time goes by. If you've created a reasonable number of posts, all of which are ranked on search engines, you can relax and begin to reap the results of your efforts.

Also, you might start outsourcing some of your activities to freelancers when you've expanded the blog to a certain stage. For starters, you might outsource keyword analysis and articles writing to freelancers so you could have room for other important aspects of your company or existence. On fiverr.com and upwork.com, you will find good freelancers.

Lightning Source UK Ltd.
Milton Keynes UK
UKHW020633080121
376670UK00015B/2003